Roots & Branches Series

CITY

a poem from the end of the world

Michael Boughn

SPUYTEN DUYVIL
New York City

Some of these poems have appeared in the following publications: *ecolinguistics, Posit, Cough, The Buffalo News, House Organ, Rampike, Trinity Review, Altered Scale, Cedilla, The Café Review, Boneshaker Anthology,* and *A Celebration of Western New York Poets. City Book One – Singular Assumptions* was first published in a slightly different form by Book Thug in 2014.

Special thanks to Victor Coleman and the crew of the bpNichol Lane Writing Group for their invaluable editorial input. Each of these bears their mark.

2016 Michael Boughn
Take what you need and leave the rest

ISBN 978-1-941550-87-8

Library of Congress Cataloging-in-Publication Data

Names: Boughn, Michael, author.
Title: City : a poem from the end of the world / michael Boughn.
Description: New York City : Spuyten Duyvil, [2016]
Identifiers: LCCN 2015044644 | ISBN 9781941550878
Classification: LCC PR9199.4.B68 A6 2016 | DDC 811/.6--dc23
LC record available at http://lccn.loc.gov/2015044644

Cover photo by Michael Boughn

for Jack

and his Charles

The World
has become divided
from the Universe. Put the three Towns
together

CHARLES OLSON, "POEM 143. THE FESTIVAL ASPECT"

Book One

Singular Assumptions

In the first Town
somebody will have addressed
themselves
to someone else.

Charles Olson, "Poem 143. The Festival ASPECT"

PART ONE

Prelude

"Space is not the setting (real or logical) in which things are arranged, but the means whereby the positing of things becomes possible."

MAURICE MERLEAU-PONTY

I.1.1 AUGURIES OF THE END

i.

Take City   (any number   sketchy signs of previous
stacked or folded)   use the story   grail maps recurrent
                gift brings to roar   of its crashing
hauling in   disturbance's   shore   inhabited domesticities
in face of streets   will not yield   coteries of sharpened
        intensifications along   hearts   intent on ravaged
            borders of vague   ponds approach   diamond
dreams of trees   shards flecked   through broken green
            margin   shadows at the edge   of frail reminding
        error calling out   distances of sagging   flesh to be home
return to   limits of   dinner escape a lurid
        insinuation's residual   tourist when there you are   no
                sailing messages   shouting rudely
however many sheets   in front of others either here
        wind past distant   or here both reeking as one
            of difference   frying onions and garlic
        not half   bad,   half
                a gift from dead   being left   to fend
reproaches at bridge of   random guesses
                ridiculous beauty   home   blood swelling
        diffidently across   dark depths of eyes' heavens
            pages of its encounters   thought's
        machine love   grinding
insistent engine roar   ruling out   nothing

ii.

Uncertain wavers   still   put this into another
       resolve   waiting   say bones
          to be sentenced   in the reading
        mirror morning   rattles behind
                shines on it that door
   no thought   real bones
   reflection   and a real City
   entering it such a thing
as islands that float   imagined
         on it   pointing
         strangely   fails it,   bones
of the lake   could be   its telling
a City   could cities   knock knock knock
        mean as little   as stones   of its telling
        as lake means   tock tick tock . . .
           to its stones?

iii.

What happens next   counterfeiting spirit
  around a corner   lacunae conundrum   iniquities
vast boxed spaces stacked   fading into smudged
            plastic   exits returned   to clover
        as China turns out   leaf violations of spatial
        enlightenment   integrity   Escher loops
    turn wheels of progress   boys in black   gather at crucial nodes
with packages of subprime mortgages   articulated dance step
                collateralized debt   embrace
        a kind of gate   abandoned   to siren's wail   shattered
            hope left   lost deep fatal divisions and false
        dust of acceleration's hierarchies phantom perfective
    inane pastures sprouting   tombs yielding   programmed desolate weed
            edge in vague   harvest on former   fields of plenty
        terrains of monstrous   dream technicians of dubious
        habitations   ghosts of swaying   character muddy water
    moan uselessly   of grid's   steady pulse   lithic desolation across divide's
            locked trauma   till   counterfeiting spirit's   renewal mirage
worked into fields   stunted   and stubbled   new discounts   proportional
        namelessness   dream extension   shadow tree
            circum-terran hunger   entering   emanation of besmirched
        grimaced   white eyed   mental operational abyss
    moon tranced howling   at tractor hindered   entrance choked
trailers and their gleaming   bumper to bumper sun
            silver maidens beckoning   glint blinding   perverse
space bound roar   of on time delivery   in haze   idling in mixed combustion
                        of what passes for air waste and packed metallic
    asphalt mazes   steaming intro to souls' crush inching downward
        interminable excretions   of self   into valley   of planetary fatality

iv.

A necessary legerdemain   dizzying   gelatinous residue
                        incarnated positions   of self-made success
                rage fixed   rudderless and amok
        greed for answers   positionality's
        certain inflection of generality   in Waynsian
hermetically sealed   tonality   facing endless waves
                of gooks in various   head gear
from another instant   till laughter
                        a slight shift   leaves it riding
        eyes sealing it   with reins between
        slick and fast   teeth into blazing
                skies   renditions of heroes
        always a problem   outcome's inevitable
                view from kaleidoscope   ingestion into ranges of storied
        high ground humans left   fading   into distances
                to claim it after inception   resembling glory
of singular business as mad   discounts at your local
                        edge of world   Walmart   this way says
                some spook trying to jack
        bodiless back to back   syntactical confusions
                in lock up remade ironies   will steal
                eating soup   point of view   leaving transfusions
        stumbling, coughing   a last retort

I.1.II THE END

for André Spears

Flames have been in the picture   sporadic but growing
                    there's no shortage   of assholes   god knows
            but certain demands   in the smog
        beyond the diamond   send signals
    to broken hearts   in dismal night
        of the last retort   indicating other
                        turns of   significant
                close patterned   but random   import disguised
            as circling's noose   or progress   asks craftily
                    to haul away   a nice noun
            they can hook   like you
        shattered   in such   a tasteless sentence
                jewels of it   grope your mind's
irrefragable departures into dreams   twisting into
        smogged out polis   phantasm   configurations of small
            hearts demanding to know   shopping pleasure
            who is what and how   cultural satisfaction
                            reaches beyond   vast collection's well-laid out
plan   turns left at the second   corridor of ease
                looking for   you are here
            landmarks   red star in the flames
gun on the seat   indicating walls
                next to the father   you have known before
        the flames   constantly within
archival matter's   floor plan progress
                    maybe it   was   ineluctably discrete
        in which case   eternal sidewalk
directions are hopeless   in anthromechanical
                        production   lockup

9

I.1.III LATER

for Guy Davenport

              Looking back knowing   closes the joint down
because looking back   is lost   to further   unrestrained jubilation
  asphalt reaches into   spread of   torsions whose limits bound
     simple widening distance   ghost whispers pain   unbearable instant's
        fierce wind whipped   erupting language   escaping declensions
cement tree tombs   and anonymous   bottleneck   yields moment's fiscal
   resolve eating   endless oil shits   erasure blotting all   thought beyond
      whole Atlantics of poison daily   scheduled grid action   monied extent
        cavernous   empty forms   obsidian obstructions
pioneering inhuman vacuum knowledge   a worrisome trend in sense of belonging
         rotten concrete brunt   indices of divorced and packaged
    plunge   dark inert sealed   fitness   for sale in
locomotive nurseries   Puffing Billy destiny   quantified determination
        flattened   viral integral dangle   in displays
      roads exfoliate   blinding type, too   moral frequencies' ferocious litanies
of ruined proportion   anemic strained   spectral pleasures render lifeless
    dead air box inward desert   asphalt music into   five obstructions
   alone contracted   paralysis highway   ardent belief youth   tyrannical   smooth
parking lot greed   levelled and paved   wrinkle free toxic yield's illusion
         world extinguished   godlike immune   verisimilitude's
annihilation chuckle   less than sovereign   writing   antiquely tormented stuff
      of renditions popular sports   encased in long streams of lights
bringing equivalent apparitions performance   red trail doom   human commuted
       product measured   into sentence's impeccable   grammatical
        car length   risk averse spatial   distillated architecture's
  fortification   disguised order   ends in brittle tellurian distraction

I.1.IV.   ARMAGEDDON

for Peter Culley

        State of excess   churning past
    incommensurable   end toward
        any sense   of long useless   dimensions
            objective   miniaturized exchange
                growing boil   into blurry sequence
    beyond control process
                to cross purposes   returns lost to ends
    impacts multiplying   endless   ecstasy
        disintegrating   beyond sacrifice
                    enormous   retardation of
            congested satiation's   indifferent creeping
                        invincible   asphalt coffin
            obese systems   floating money rings
        messages   beyond earth of no
            hope of   value   exhausted
        meaning clogged   pierced and bleeding
    air fouled excretions   oil seeping   into dead seas
        machinic   triumph   and chromosomal
    desolate time   memory   lingering
            in air-conditioned   cellular archipelagos
                    of intelligence`s   Sargasso dream

I.1.v. THE FINAL APOCALYPSE, REALLY
for Victor Coleman

You don't amount   to chemically induced
                hill of   youth   trumps chemically
assumed valueless   revealed gods   in strict
        legumic rendition   contraction   of other
                        messy   lessons
    in the price of gas   and how to die   you
                remains the stuff   of discounted
    wild introspection   or a semi portion
        leaving the dust   of common traction
                    to settle symbolically   in constant terminal
ennui patterns   fits designed   satiate
        fields of berries   provide   new itches   also indicate
            stuff of dream's stores   closed early
    when inevitable excretions   of home went
                tripping   botox babe on arm
        to Walmart to open   patrolling vectors
                untold dimensions   of intractable denial
    and deferred satisfactions   wreathed in late night
        audience responsibility   vigils in tenebrous
                    context implications   leave
        yielding apparitions   penultimate apocalypse
                in wildest dream   yearning for more
                    induced clamour   torrid encounters
    contribute to factors   of viral disasters
            establishing happy   and bellicose arsenals
possible contributions   to reason   in desire's
                circumstance's   gently scented boudoir
        and green and hilly   resolutions

I.1.VI AFTERWARDS

for Meredith Quartermain

terminal affirmations   smooth fenders ineffable curve into vectors of speechless
accelerate beyond toward   power repackaged
flesh in metallic ecstasies   for later viewing
parking lots' ease extended   familiarity   leisure of foreshortened
specimen redwoods   jolt's various invasions
and wheels for salvation   unsecured real estate leaves behind
incognito destined   axiomatic armour   chagrin   does not do justice   does not reach
late morning's   eternal   glinting depths of fallen regimes   disruption
exclamation outside   implied production   of smooth zooms
death's lost venue   panning across stacked ramps
sibylline lapses   lead extreme inertia into   arching declarations
desiccated but happy   autonomous illusions
extension's optical   interred in frozen
trajectories   the world   vocabulary's nominal
disappears   taking yesterday   moral paradigm   requiring rejuvenated
with it   then arrival   stacked multitudes astride
kicks ass   arterial exactitudes
left in dark its making rarely   feeds into hungry attractors
surpasses   asphalt streams   ruins of real
lurid wounds   inflicted   care looking   like some detailed
vehicular claim   exquisite execution
of music   ecstasy   speed   timed to coincide
with erotic   automatisms in folded   plies of vision   dreams of ill defined escape clause
machine's rendition   drifting among endless versions
of little deuce coup   red lights flashing
love in the flow of its   doom corridor

Part Two

Rush Hour

"Psyche is extended, but knows nothing about it."

Sigmund Freud

I.2.1   EGLINTON AT 5

It's never through with you, never
done with the deaths original
to your own figurations
of happy trails or another

stroll through the garden
of shattered hearts, pieces
crunching under relentless
reflections on the nature

of metaphysics. Examined
traffic patterns yield
crusading misprisions in place
of flows when deflect

enters the picture. When the picture
enters deflect confusions
confound patterns claim
to assigned seat. The light

changes and no one moves
because distant incursions
of injected greed breeds
entropic fixations normal

stasis and no one really wants
to get there knowing pensioned
conclusions offer little hope
beyond brief visits to distant

unapproachable worlds
of bad teeth, crushed goats
writhing in dust, and another
beautiful day in the light

stolen from time at a cost
calculable only in utter
disregard for what passes
for decency, a concept ripped

from pages of unique
literary merit. Repeated adjectival
superlatives ring bells
in alien belfries rousing objections

anticipated well before approaches
to various ramps announce
impassable blockades of jammed
up steel and rubber founding economies

of pain and routine passages
through unthought habits against blank
skies of late February. Food
and roof wander into labyrinth's

multitude of reasons and become
stone. Not stoned, which would reopen
negotiations with traffic patterns
toward possible, what? entropic

fibrillations or analogical
eruptions into parking lots across
GTA, little gestures of love oozing
into front seats with hot pizza

after game's folderol? Sheer unlikeliness
of the sky caught up in rivers
of red lights, silent and still
over stabilized motion interruptions

stretching into fields of grief
for unrecognized iron fortune's
rendition of *almost there if it
weren't for the damned traffic*

announcements leave it *likely*, in fact
newsworthy for broadcasts
across temporal grid interstices
every night at six while economies

quiver thinking of arrangements
opening, beginning to move
into the night, shifting constellations
flowing toward another long day.

I.2.11   No beer

"Beer is proof that God loves us and wants us to have fun."
—Benjamin Franklin

Hidden horizons are a dime
a dozen when essences
drop their drawers

in stunning displays of rare
rectitude's bare life. If
cheeky doesn't quite expose

hidden things to adequate
scrutinies, inward forms
will. It is the ascending

that gets stuck in the craw
when any old will do
if only you get

the joke. Converging lines
of extremely *tenuous*
are a kind of punch
woven out of wheelbarrows
and oceans into ways
to get by when the face

of the bay, moods scintillant
across its skin, speaks
only to calculations

of exterior triangulation's
contracted rectal retentions
disguised as a sure

thing. No beer is then enough
to reset severe seismic
interpenetrations that leave

town as quickly as time
allows. Where amid I
drifts through recurrent

anthems and thirsty
penguins where beer
is known to occur

among dripping window's
revelations of weekly
prowess and endless

interpretations of bounce
and calls provides escape
from silenced halls of misplaced

splendor. Small consolations
count, but sometimes even beer
is not enough to make up

for desolations intimate insistence
on stop time encounters'
extensions into bakeries

of human stupefaction, though
never forget the first thing we
did was invent beer, knowing

even then that Isis had a plan
anticipating Benjamin
Franklin. If god wants us to have

fun, no beer is a real sign
of analogical incursions' rendered
aether reeking of ontic

regulators and theo-shit
kickers. Woe to joyful anticipation
when the knock comes and it is time

to pay up, at least as far as that figures
in economies of intended outcomes
and fair game pasted across the back

of any erratically moving thing
across paved expanse of remarkably
consistent anti-vaginal terrors.

1.2.III SHELF LIFE

Predictable death replaces thrill
drunk plunge into temporal
depths when automat regulated

selections' non-celestial bread
pudding rules. Annunciation
of interiors ticking clock leads

to inevitable distractions
and injections of righteous
names of immaculate health,

the same one subjects obey
in endless reductions of non
construed salivations implying

subtle bodies of succulent
persuasion. Flush it reels beyond
sense of hard won, elusive

form's clinging to stellar
recessions. Disposal becomes
anxiety's certain fading

nightmarish order extension
into art and desiccated meters reeling
from sober intoxications

and infinitude intrusions
render streets perpendicular
to any intended claim to spontaneous

topographical coitus left
gasping alone with metrical-moral
traditions in a small room reeking

of groves and subjected to rigorous
reductions of potential wrong
turns. Judgment, all dolled up

for the ball gets dumped with coded
impositions of necessary
hungers to the beat of daily

skim. Forgetting the stars leaves hell
on wheels as normative condition. Best
before end times coagulates in repeated

anticipation demands relentless use
devouring mountains and other
potential products as a matter

of sacred imperative. Move along
is the sound it makes while brightness
remains mutual signature's

elusive visibility in edges
dulled from yesterday's demand
for another new container just

like the last one, expecting true greatness
within syntactical determinations
and peer-reviewed short lists. A sure thing

if you know the right people
perched on the edge of fame, basking
in glory of time stamped success

and prizes galore, a veritable
midway of potential pay-offs
dangling like over ripe peaches

in a bad simile. Then your due date
starts to flash, anticipating
retirement with full pension to some

newly drained Florida lot, temporal
shutdown closing in according
to schedule determined in distant

laboratories of compulsory time
regulation, *regular* sneaking
in to register rule's ascension

to invisible hand's regal
inheritance disguised as human
but with middle finger extended.

I.2.IV PISSING ON THE BURNING BUSH IN THE NAME OF EFFICIENCY

Moments of uncomfortable revelation
indicate City has been penetrated
over a barrel. The bush bursting

into flame lights up paths of flowered
approach to generosity of uses
only to be met by loud claims from angels

of wealth for open access to all
avenues of ingress. The burning
bush speaks of storm's sudden force beyond

thoughts of anger, intensity, or even mere
molecular movement as it suddenly
levels entire towns in its passionless

homage while angels of efficiency demand
reductions in plenitude and unsanctioned
occupations. Burning bushes have been known

to interrupt multiple efficiencies
designed to pull wool over ocular
occurrences of unauthorized

angularities. In any case, if you
don't look too close, as they say, which may
require increasing pressure on your onus

to neutralize repeated eruptions
of wild sense, lack of balance
produces palpable imitations

of acentric advances in realms
of fiscal assurances the whole thing
will continue past its due date

as determined in distances of insatiable
grasp. Belief is a three hundred fifty
pound monkey on your back, especially

when lights go off for a few days. Then
flaming shrubs signal City's delicate
negotiation with rampant

appetites for immediate
access and free parking next to the show's
door. Filled with hunger

for representation star gazing shifts
to throat cutting in immediate blink
of ice and fear. Whatever the bush has to say

in the name of moony tribulations
cannot translate into goods and services
or power play goals. Hence, vulgar intimations

of uncomplicated definition wrested
from lunar confusions only confirm
worst fears of inspectors

charged with regulating
episte-pathologies recognizable
in the harsh glare of reason as it

sprinkles doubt on the fire. The other
cities waver in moonlight, wondering
why the fire sputters, as if belief

as a function of established penetration
mechanisms always leads to contests
of inordinate suppression geared

toward further acquisition of human
incursion areas leave bushes bereft
of ignitable options in face of their asphalt aspect.

I.2.v THE WAR ON THE CAR

War and car don't rhyme
though you'd never know it
by looking. Having formed

every square and passage to its
wheels, asphalt and cement sock
sewn tight, imposed angular

bound vision into knotted
contortions leave limbs
wrenched, dislocated, cramped

shadows of known reach, each inch
twisted out of vehicular
contractions of morphogenetic

plenitude into rigor of its
intersections, each one timed out
of squared seconds stacked laterally

across expanses of imagination's
former self, dark formulations
of encounter rising from ashes

of place, declarations of war ring
with sardonic amplifications
of victorious erasure's contempt

for the loser who looks first
right, then left (except in England's
green pastures) and steps

into it. Sometimes it's a river
of asphalt. When the shape
of water is lost, the war enters

a new phase, waxing gibbous
in pedestrians' minds and the dreams
of commuters waiting

for the light to change. Ghosts
of entire forests wail but war
is already beside the point since world

that ended remains without adequate
ventilation leaving this one with its
lavender and lilac floating on what

can only be considered a very subtle
inflection with little credibility
beyond fading claims of necessity

and undulations of blue to fend
for itself with no chance of sure
footing. Hephaestus may step

out of the truck, squat and blunt,
dip the key in oil and fire the ignition,
but who sees him and where can you go

when the nets drop in badly rhymed
imitations of real streets, impassable
idea of *rush,* a declension of *free way*

as it plays out in sluggish rivers of red
in the night, stalled light. Meanwhile,
the war returns when hordes of cycles

descend on City out of the north
an important sign of further
origins than the regular

ones. The cars, taken by surprise,
roll back before two-wheeled bell
ringing berserker onslaught.

Regrouping at Holts, they emit
an impassable wall of carbon
monoxide lays waste to every

living thing around, leaving marauding
cycles down and scattered across endless
asphalt sweep. The cars win the war

driving back and forth over mangled frames,
twisted tires, honking and squealing
their all-weather Michelins. A national

Automobile Appreciation Day is declared
and everyone has an extra fill-up on the Mayor
before resuming their place in line.

I.2.VI   EMERGING PATHOGENS

Emerging pathogens of imaginal
substance between layers of ocular
condensation counter large scale

migrations to Costco and other
sentences of indeterminate
resolution machines count down

and flesh comes to attention. Arrows
do that, green depths of unacceptable
platitudes bending flows to paths

of patrolled rectitude indications
all's clear though risk remains active
among less than favourable

conditions for disciplinary
success and unanticipated
rest stops popping up in embarrassing

proximity to recent news of more
new ones. How it's done reckons swerve
as a kind of infection all's well deems

sketchy among angled vectors
and rigid similes because it reeks
of accident figured in terms

of non-negotiable encounters
out of the blue, into the dark, round
midnight, hour of slippery

dispensations opening into surprise
visits across the Bay's face or street's
turn that brightens colour's sudden

speech. Dying birds can be a problem
sudden slam against it leaves flutter
and flop its mute sign, immense

knowledge in small, black eyes, but what else
opens beyond contracted net's
mall cave, the otherwise of colour's

announcement of light or initiation
of each note explodes into music's
difference. That's infection enough

a word whose disrepute in climates
of rampant due dates is well-known
to regulatory modalities, to tincture

darkest opportunities with subtle
shades of blue, green, yellow, red, thus turning
on the light. Seeing it suddenly as it

sees you, pathway into the woods. Vectors
figure largely in conversations
about how to stop it before emerging

turns into unacceptable images
whose *mundus* has been known not only
to ignore rules, but to make them

dance, claiming as it does to call
to mind ground of transparent media
known to lead to unauthorized roses

and thought of red hyacinths begins
to disrupt established traffic patterns
leaving sudden openings adrift, floating

in azure air, gods from old poems cut loose
into current razzle dazzle
confusion leaves vectors without transport.

PART THREE

Entertainments

". . . our sense of an unattained self is not an escape from, it is rather an index of our commitment to the unattained city, one within the one we sustain, one we know there is no good reason we fail to attain."

STANLEY CAVELL, *CITIES OF WORDS*

I.3.1 ARENAS I HAVE KNOWN

Insert more coins angelic machine
announces through dim light at dawn
of another contest. Insert more

coins attends poverty of tentative
condition mistaken for real
furrows gravely across fields

of inattention. Heidegger equivocates
around tables of muted radiance
in the braying and unique

murmur's pulse of any crowd
over Leafs' game. Insert
more ontic resources at will

and crowding becomes intelligible
evidence of rockem sockem
glaze unmoored and slithering

across icy attentions to diverted
compositions of evaporating
being, a word often avoided

in poems of serious intent
but here indicating unbreakable
moments of fixed stares and a lack

of poetic gravitas, almost as if bizarre
insertions rendered coherence
a kind of floozy at the bar

in hazy light, bright lips ready to meet
moment's opening with a thrust
and grip in interest

of painted finish. Profound is as
profound does within the boards
of limited deflections. Then the flood

and the fun begins. Antic works
too, in nuances of varied destabilizing
confusions leave ontic skittering

through reasonable's interpretation
of icing, an indeterminable
violation of spatial propriety

known to leave aspects in apoplectic
disarray heaping abuse from stands
of authentic rage regarding lack

of blood grounded measure, knowledge
final score wreaks on obstinate
circulations yielding more glazed

and unobtrusive ordinations
and arrangements of antic
fibrillation. Insert more compassion

is a kind of nagging nudge
toward chasms of sudden eyes
in the glare of chronic temporal

condensation. Repetitions of no
fixed address indicate itinerant
applications of self-enclosed

limits leave regular's tattered regalia
even more shredded. What else is there
along endless boulevard of shops

leading destiny into small, desperate
payments in hope some claw
may return *technē* to intimacies

of familiar names and common
untranslatable embraces beyond *they*
toward final period's inevitable buzzer

1.3.11 A PARADE OF STOOPING POETS

The weight of each letter
burdens equals with slouched

intentions on view. Machinations
abound, fluency of political

forms yielded in dark
privacies of sweeping

gesture's storied incandescence
evaporate into *pet*

petit exclamations of avant
garde pope master

satisfaction. Sufficient
detached riots of appropriate

disgrace count, and weight
of directional intent to bear world's

collapsing columns of social
capital emancipated in pains

taking attention to bear. Emerging
advances may yield formulas

of relieved stress raising
livelihoods beyond extensions

of mere poetic commerce
into investments of major

yields, or at least minor
empires of sometimes crumbling

authorities reconstituted
in satisfactory dispensations

of reading allotments and eventual
park place rent thing, not

that other rent with its
difficult openings, but

the one that goes ka ching
having translated indigestible

into toll house minus the butter,
the point being advanced

toward dues collections and cards
announcing admission to herd

of independent minds booked
for some corner of the next MLA

convention out of deep need
to be there. Being there

is a function of spectacular
incursions of antithetical

density in spectral forms of peer
reviewed ectoplasmic ideosubstance

not exactly the mind Waldo dreamed
when cities of words flowed

from distant rivers into those mouths
at the edge of the sky but a damned

good way to become subject
of or to the *Maddening Zug Island*

Hum, that universal drone eruption
into conference's interminable

expression of spectacle's grip
on the *cajones* of every little notion

I.3.III   GLOBAL WARMING VS. TEXAS

Where belief stumbles is faced
with technocracies of abundant
density holed up in innumerable
brains where it weighs down

lighter elements with ponderous
observations and largely concealed
weapons designed to equalize
any errant discriminations

democracy has failed to render
into products worthy of weekly
attention and extreme acts of attenuated
credit. Tenuous atmospheres

leave vision fixated in singular
messes, lone stars burning brightly
over parched stretches of desiccated
ground where half a billion trees

take a right to the kisser
floors them for the count, the rest
left staggering while Texas, dancing
back and forth over skewed limbs

announces its intention
to execute all remaining evasions
of self-administered lobotomy
procedures to protect and preserve

legitimate archonic aspects
yielding molecular rearrangements
of visionary materials into shop
windows lavishly outfitted

with genuine imitations
of identical jackets or boots
designed to generate real
outbursts of lollapalooza

shit kicking and other enthusiastic
patriotisms. It's a hell
of a country and no indications
to the contrary can produce

vision beyond super-sized
satisfaction's gaudy projections
of temperature controlled four hour
erections stabilizing the drive

home. The drive home doesn't like
global warming either, but it doesn't
hit it. It does complain
about the weather which Texas

finds subversive. The Alamo
then shows up, confused about its
contextual significance, but always
game for a slugfest with whomever

is around. Remembering it
is not it, and perhaps that's why
global warming is laid out amid
limbs of all those forgotten

trees. Remembering leads
to sudden ejaculations of manhood
the sticky kind affectionately
recalls correctly positioned

last stands and other tableaus of pumped
up vacuity hungry for a fight
with anything moves. After all
oceans do rise from time to time

and need to be slapped
down just to show them who's boss
around here. Around here quivers at thought
of more feats of engineering prowess

extending into its flows and quietly
leaves through the back door taking
global warming with her
into dank alley's storied egress.

I.3.iv ECONOMIC REALITY

"I don't need therapy – I need money."
student saying

You can't earn enough in most
lifetimes to pay for the poetry
required to explain economics
to reality. If words could be worn

out and used up, crinkled in small
soiled balls or left emptied
and sticky in hornet infested
containers, economic reality

would be its *tractatus*, its ode
on a Grecian liar
ringing through hulls of democratic
bluster from mouths in swollen

red faces determined to pull
bootstraps of every errant pilgrim
into gravy free enterprise
of incarnate logos saturated

dispensation's spiritualized
saving accounts. Who remembers
economics is to home as divine
life is to distant archaeology

of theological midden heap
may be prepared for sudden
showings forth of hidden doors'
transgalactic transfer of cold

words into apparitions of deeper
encounter. Say, a parking lot
within the one you just left
your car in, a vast sealed tomb

vibe emanating into corners
and crevices while it rides
a reputation for ease of shopping
pleasure, free parking, and

authorized admission. Then economic
reality realizes the rent
is too low and moves increase of what
ever margin darkness brings to talk

of blue. Household debt, too
a mystery of subtle encounters
with manifestations of density
deficit, misses the train and winds up

trapped in an allegory of profligate
burghers astride equine
rectitude in the charge up
Consumption Hill. Gravy

as elemental leads to formations
of fat cutting and periodic
weigh ins designed to distract
attention from vacuous visions'

hallucinatory underground utopia
toward what people want and back.
What people want is an abyss
yawning with boredom and often

confused with questions of life
on other planets. Is it there? and how
many eyes does it have? Economic
reality is its human disguise

amid levers of power and stands
for distribution of terror and pain
beyond the usual kind, along with
accumulations and hordes beyond

as they say, imagining, where all gravy
goes once it has been cut, or cut
loose, a true economic reality
awash in glory and righteous

affirmation of divine law, or
maybe just a general rule
or possibly an operating
principle, anyway how fat

always flows, as part of the Grand
Design, up, which is where after all
it belongs, in immaculate
dough-re-mi ascensions

I.3.v   Rehabilitating the true iamb

The once upon a time world formerly
known, or at least spoken in turns

of inadequate formulation, as resting
on blocks of hygienic precisions

yields a certain panache of unruly
hilarity in corners and cracked

terrain. The embrace is a thing
encountered in mercury lit

parking lots deep in the spread of night
angled encounters and flows

where the vibes thin into well-made
laminar hymns. Both aspects

afire begs the analogy
for clarity, though particular incursions

leave such intendant caretakers
in the midst of the only question

that matters when funny
no longer occupies a declension

of thinking but usurps all modal
intricacies and variations leaving dead

parrots in charge of transit and other
municipal distractions. But that's

politics, and metrics, too, which brings us
back to the true iamb, that wily old

fart riding the air flow into relentless
articulations of cloud logic's worst

nightmare. The need for rehab
arises out of heavy insinuations

of irregular toxic inculcations
by rhythmic deviants related

to overly intimate associations
with atonal breaches in the historical

fabric. Wastelands of varying
density hang out behind curtains

demanding to be heard, claiming
redemptive associational

immunity from the tumult
continues to stir shit up

in anticipation of new shades of blue's
signature. They like the view and the sign

is well-written, explaining in clear
prose natural determinations

of pedal misnomers and how instants
of singular rhythmic contraction

uphold civilization's virtuous claim
to keep the hips calm. Stressed out

is related if you think about it
in terms of a kind of moral

rictus, a silent scream in the face
of some ambiguous young beat

strutting its stuff in wanton displays
of variable feet's projective

razzamatazz leaves the metrical
moral tradition not just aghast

but straining after the idea of order
as key to furthering common decency's

demand for more prisons and regular
bowel movement's reassuring fragrance

I.3.VI NO FURTHER ADIEU

Having reached the end returns godly
reminiscences to orginary impulse's

boundary fetish. Maybe not boundary
as breath on neck announces

skin – more like a fence through dappled
meadow, a real fence, no doubt, but reeking

of overripe metaphors. Relief of the end
is a kind of meadow and therefore

dappled, a state of interruption tumbling
out of the trees, some of which are oak,

birch, and sugar maple, at least
as memory has it. Wind telegraphs it

and edges flutter, delight a question
best left hanging, a state suspended

in light of dappled meadow
which may take tautology to a level

of impertinent signals, the kind
that lose you or leave you overlooked

by the mainstream which is busy
reiterating pre-established cartological

conundrums ironically inflected
to indicate subtle distances and taste

for Great Literature. If it bids
awakening, it remains a silent

partner, though the stakes become
astronomical, translated into blue

light of stars whose distances wheel
along boundary *adieu* calls

to attention, to here, that supple
shift of weight yields the world

in spades. Anyway, it's a place to start
infrequent engagements with enormous

instances of lapsed, terminal nostalgia
thus getting on with it, no further

being a prod because certain limits resist
easy placement. Returning to delight's

surprising instance was ordained
by virtue of some difficult

to define authority often
omitted from list of admissible

proclivities. But maybe further
interrupts it, leaves it behind

and delight is cut loose, maybe
no further's boundary leaves *adieu*

in the dust of a passage delight
claims to have elaborated in clear

flutters signalling another City
not so much beyond as within, the way

a dream is within the arms of nether,
a boundary of such disproportionate

nebulosity as to make a Bay
blush, 5AM, July 4th, two thousand

twelve, and then it *is* breath on neck
announcing skin even as the fence

continues to demand its dispensations
and formations, and the meadow

shakes off metaphorical implications
and dapples as if life depended on it

BOOK TWO

Other climates

In the second Town
the earth
will have replaced
the sun.

CHARLES OLSON, "POEM 143. THE FESTIVAL ASPECT"

PART 1

End of Regulated Area

"The City redefined becomes a church. A movement of poetry. Not merely a system of belief but their beliefs and their hearts living together."

JACK SPICER, "A TEXTBOOK OF POETRY"

II.1.1.   PARTED FIRES

Infinite recession's
                        slightly parted
lips burden
         city with wet

        raptures of between
                           leaves high
and dry
longing for some
            firm ground
to plant
        roses in—ridiculous
bounces around
too, disturbance beyond reach
                               parted implies, noting
        very small
        movements bring
        down empires

at least as far
        as disturbance reminds
        effects of hardens
        rippling through layers
diaphanous suggestions
                   of parted,
a mouthful
of unexpected death
at the edge of City

Not just dark
                    hole full of sense
wet, slight
                    pressure tracing
passages
                    beyond unbroken
interpretation's certain
                    homecoming

                                        Simple flows
            hopelessly,
and credulous song drifts
            through confusions
of diaphanous

not so much boundless
            as unable to end
                                parted
                                in songs
                                        Grosser
bodies of thought thrust
            angels into clean
            and reverent
            codes
but parted quanta
            let them in
            whole, their flight

an indigestible query
                            regarding
dark and wet outcomes
                            regarding
body's ridiculous wasting
                            regarding
            parted fires heat
            young men die for

Angel slips
        shadow to shadow
                empty streets
                peering through parted
     tongues stumbling
over quickened
and parted as
      distances fill it
          and City wakes
to light
and another day

II.1.II UNAUTHORIZED VEHICLES

"All unauthorized vehicles will be towed at owner's expense."
The State

Intricate affections
                                        of dead wood
in parks of white
                                city's arrival. No

agony or flat
                                tires, just
calculations of pearl
                                now Jack's
                                        Pearl, that swinging
translation's supposition
                        of smooth
                                        flanks
                                        its hold on
such gorgeous interruptions
                        and violations
                                of doom's
                                                vowel's
dark prognostication

Gnostic adumbration
                                        strung through branches
                        such a beginning
return to a way
                        toward relief

It might be more
                        in some end
as desire for living

                              trees, though expense
of spirit always
                    furthers columns
                    demand for bottom
                    line's muzak and random
                                             constructions resemble
souls. Trees
             carry on
             as if no matter
             of fact signified
beyond spring

                    Spring
doesn't mean it
             but carries on
             anyway
             it can

It's all going
             to end drifts
among birch till wind
             shifts, waves rise

It's all
             a matter of fact
lost in wind's
             direction turns
waves to frequencies
             within repeated
attempts to mean
             dismissal's dismal

suggestion

Wind's *veers*
      indicates further
heavens open
      into small parks, gathered
                strangers regaling
      stories of
        wild sprees
          in street's angular
      rectitude, regulated
      crossing and minimal
      regalia
        But unauthorized
      vehicles still enter
      perpendicular injunctions
           holding
           out hope
           at arm's length
while keeping a watch
      on strict temporal
      dispensation's return
          painted grey, mounted
          on poles to receive
          offerings for minutes
          doled out on credit

Years pass
springs and winds fall
      from skies
        of untold
        reckoning. Unauthorized
waves of rising
      encounter leave here
          to struggle
            beyond the sock

                                        of its daily bread
beyond
        authorized vehicles'
                              immaculate
deception and righteous
                        claim to Faust's invention
of matter as idol
                or atomic bomb
                                claiming
dominion over literal
                        interpretations while stones
                                masquerading as imminent
exactitudes
of dream
            speak, remarking
boundary   reels
                from too many shots
                                to the head
and a solemn
                legislative malfunction

II.1.III EMPIRES OF VAPOUR

Among Dupont's scattered wounds
                                    ragged commercial
edge, sudden curve
                    of attention shaped
                                    to cocked hip
draped in thought. Small
                    blessing opens drama
                    of exceptional light
without benefit
                    of a single belief, no
strings attached
                            She
doesn't even know
                    just that sweep
                    of thigh is full
                    of dream, in
habitation, strange ground
                            with no fixed
                                        address, nothing
                                        tied to scheduled arrivals. City's
concrete examples built
                    of codes that hold
                    limits in further
                    dramas of skies offering
                    exceptional currency, as charge
flows through Bloor's
                    afternoon roar, sudden blue
                                    through sun flashed towers

Then it's just
you, me and the next

                           corner where sympathy
of earth and sun plays
                    out
                           in transitive intimations
of further elations
                    among stellar events
and distribution of cruelty
                           remains a matter
of attention to news
                    of another
                    dead child
                    starved, beaten
just down the street

So much a part
      of us
      a plural pronoun
      containing
Second Town's becoming
                           animal crossing into asphalt
extensions down edge
                    coyote trails sweep through
                    along curve of riparian
memories urban rent
                    green slash through towers'
delusion

Hard to figure
                    such implicate energies in odd
corners of soul
                    studded with fall's ragged
corridors
leaf litter

Clouds that suggested
                    elaborations of ocular command
and a return to loins
                  of the visible are buoyed
by hot luminescence
               in storied distances
between roofs
          still fill eyes
                with folds and shadows
announce billows
            of time
                amid thought
of City's face

          promise sweeping
          across it from the end
          out

II.1.IV OTHER SECTORS' SELF-REGULATING COMPLIANCE

"Who's number one?! Who's number one?!"
John Berryman

The story of City
                passes itself
                                on the 401
weird verbal jackknife leading to multiple
collusions of temporal
intent
        a general
circulation modulates
                        into rivers of red
sluggish lights
            flashing
            warnings
            of imminent
            shut down

Then authentic voices
                reaffirm expressive
                                output's greatness within

limits prescribed
                by soft shoulders
                                sudden lane
closures
        Set backs
go with the ground
                and pathologies
are hard to miss
                in mazey detours
through real
        rocky terrain

Picking
       has to do
       with discriminations of shattered
                        words
                        verbal
                        detritus
                        scattered
           across swaths
             of tattered
               stories

each stone
           rosined with song
                   of exceedingly rare
                          earth

The thought
           is blue
           surging
           white caps on a
sidewalk where it
              shoulders through crowds
                      through eye's flash
                      thump of flesh
art of lost
           idiom's
             interpretations
of twanging
gut, breath
on reed, splash
of pigment, leave
             compliance adrift
                    in evidentiary deficits
                          masquerading as stones
with no song
           to bind City's passages

                                        towers, nodal
                                        intensities
spell out further
                          arrangements of internal
combustion

Flames querulous
                          here flickers
liquid release thick
                    blue orange
                                        licking unbound
into storied noise
ethereal arenas
                    reek of each
                    name imposed
                                        on perfection's sudden
rent fabric, torn
                          rectitude's command approach
to non-linear frictional
interactions
                    Elusive
laughter leaves
                    at or *with* in celestial
                                        combat for determinations
of civic outcomes
resolving pyramidal
                          ascension
into promiscuous
                    intermissions
                                        of joyous racket
while City waits
          for the time between
          time's end and the time
          after to open
its heart

II.1.v   GRANULAR MATTER

Distinguished inclusion's indirections
                    are a matter
                    of difficult predictions

                                        Birds arrive
straw filled robin's beak
                            answering to stories
                                                of birds
Perfect timing means message
shows up

            as a matter of fact, a fact
            of matter, not some cheap

parlour trick, notwithstanding
                            absent parlour. Then the hearse
                            arrives out of
                                        nowhere, falls
                            in behind
all the way to Hammer Street
                            leaving accumulations
                            of shadow to drift
                            under a dark, flattened
                            dome

                            Granular
irritation grinds
            too soothing into reticulation
            of sore elbow, oozing
            ankle, a memo
regarding tragic digressions' inability
                                to contain unauthorized vehicular
interaction and explosive
mnemonic charge

driving dissipative systems beyond
                              drifting into new
arrangement of chaotic
                    response's fallout
                                    Ah, those
were the days
              of unrestrained
verbal exuberance
                    and promiscuous
diction

              Rising song's no time
                        a real hullaballoo
                        of unbound earth's insistent
                        solar disruption,
                                    that flash
of charity
              a strange word to appear
              here
                        but bearing generosity
into between
                    so that matter
thickens
              even as it rises on

o god how not to say gossamer

then stings
              the enchainment
                              untoward moment
of gratuitous orange
                        water's murmur
                        through stone's tender
                        throat, City's silence

in peach streaked dawn, never
having seen it coming

But names
        of the oligarchs
        are matters
        of record yielding
        spectacle of inevitable
        sale known to rouse
        capillary turpitude fulfilling

league's penance race renders
                          ordinary game
                                of local lots
                                into avenue's routes
through any number of hearts
laid low

      Lined up
at the bar
        displays of digital
                connections disguised
                as home

on the range, a stubborn need
for place before even content's
                        imagined reformation
bellied up to commercial
                        encounters otherwise dumb
failures engage in possible
                        though improbable conjunctions
along mutual meridians
                        of history's
demarcations

Eating alone

watching speed's blur and roar across sun's
glare over subtle tones
                        of nachos and departing
                        desire while everyone wonders
                        who
will win the game

                    Vague recognitions
flicker through perspectives scattered
across those conversations
                            with night

but expected corner
                    fails to meet leaving
                    calculation
                    to wander obscurely
among illuminated
                    shapes *suggest themselves*
                                        in struggle to see
final articulation proceeding
                            in general direction
                            of setting
                            sun
hoping for transformations
                            imagining
a language calls out
                    to insurgent shapes
                    demanding an end
                    of prizes and spectacles of self
congratulatory content for sale
                                to spectres
dead to the prospect

                                    Flickering
glimmers announce no
rise or fall
                    just an edge
                    of City's vocabulary
stutters specificity
of imminent closure

II.1.VI EVADING SURVEILLANCE

"The Person can neither be deduced nor explained."
Henry Corbin

The City limits have been known
in impositions of contracted

dreaming to writhe

                    Pain follows
though necessarily ahead
                         new distances
open it into

               hence
                    before
                         now
begins again
and this time
                    meaning
                    henceforth space
                    music makes out
                    of traffic with figures
                    of stone

beneath asphalt. Who`s watching
                              the store takes on
new meaning
                    new
sense of thickened
               location, as if retrograde
molecular rearrangements
                         anticipating questions lead
                                   to evasive action

Most demands won`t validate
                              twists of logic
                              the same way
moon does at 4AM
                    Bathing in it
                    leads luminescence
                                        into winding queries, a City
of no mnemonic collonades
                              but still moments
embraced by pale
                    light slips into elusive
passages evaporating
                         figures lurk in the roil holding
back reluctant to name
                              new streets in light
of day knowing solar
                         infestations can raise modal
oscillations recompose letters
                              resemble angels
easily confused
with *names of rising forth*

                         Improprieties
abound where property slips
into improper confusions
of placement
                    The watcher
not so easily misled
                         avoids civic conundrums regarding
other
        possible
                    conclusions

Propitious signage
                    is no use
                    having been deployed

              along regulated routes
                                    around obstacles
to foregone agreements

                  It's a question
of seeing broken in whatever
                  potential remains unobserved
                  but just a bit different

                                    Evasive
pales into thought
                  of moonlight as a measure
                  of trembling's unlikely
                  but sweet resolution
                                    into finite lamentation for another
lost figure of completion

                  If its face
                  lingers forever
between, is it?
                  A precinct zoned
            for indistinction, dance
                        of flickering shadow
                                          in dim light of alley empties
            darkness into prospective
            formations threaten to bust open
            the night?

                  The tone
shifts toward registers of doom
even as earth
catches fire and angels mount
trees to announce
                  new verges

PART 2

Anonymous homonymies

"We are engaged on a mission: we are called to give shape to the earth."

NOVALIS

II.2.i Licking the window

If you put the cell
                                on wheels, call it
antelope
does the road
go somewhere?

                        When everything's here
                        but officials demand
                        regular deliveries of pre-approved
                                                            credit lines, distinctions
between enclosures rest
                                on selling no product beyond
                                                            a logo yet to come

Such potential leaves
                                City bound and trussed
                                                            before want's intractable window
delivers parades of stuff oozes
                                        meaning dosed
                                                            applications of pheromones
leave the current crop of homonyms
                                                strangely bereft of illegitimate variables
                                                                                    begging for more
Drifting
                from one anonymous homonymy
                to another, on the other hand
                leaves well enough alone
                                        Then enough
hungry for more
                        takes control
of the sentence till there's consensus
                        enough is enough

That window
is full of secretions of often
misunderstood frivolity
indulgent in distinct populations
of verbal commotion

Dust
of the air and perfume
of sense linger in lascivious
proximity to the vacuum
of its eyes even as rising tide
of hyperbole sweeps through joy
of flowing connections render
relation unequipped and burning
for undefined but necessary
development
When quarried
sunlight mounts elusive banks
of cloud, they wobble, and when
gloire rises in concrete
examples toward solar attractors, wobble
reaches frequency inherent in any
destabilization worth
its salt
Banking on that
only increases chance mood
will overtake reasonable declarations
of limited intent and open other
wise regulated passages to permeable
hilarity
Are we on the inside
or outside?
That's a query
only licking can begin
to engage –
one City in another suddenly

shows forth
           glows. Otherwise
                         is the figure of its blink. Then
music rising. *When* is it
                never seems to find footing amid
                                 rubble, as if some roads
don't matter – or matter only
                  within habits unfolding sentence
                             imposed on repeated offences against
unruly outbursts of more
shining through –
            Davenport's angular
            portage through the King's
            Grid, or the seventeenth
            century, Jack said, through us
all
    Muted radiance in the music brings
                        windows open to passing
in it

    Gloire of an ice
                rapt maple, lunacy of sun
                        burning in crystals outside
Betty's door
            In any case, blink
            and it's there, aflame, and then
            bark again

What is a City
            if not a gathering of beggared
                        imaginations colonized by seamless
dreams tapping their feet to
                  musick, musick, musick? What
                         shines through, delicious and dripping
with thought of further displays
                dreams of tectonic rupture

                    Rapture

                              almost slips in solipsistic

                                             interruption but finds no hold

to root phonemic misdirection

                    in. Anyway, broken contingencies

                                        save the day every time, flashing

garish displays to passing

                    intimation's mortal encounter

                                        with night visitors

Are we in

          or out still doesn't matter if the lick

                                   is reconfigured in image of inconclusive

arbitration with harbingers

                    of not

                              The window reeks

of peppermint, reorganizes itself

                    as a mirror and promptly

                    disappears into its own

                    gaping proposition of some

                    previously unsuspected reflection

                    of rabbit

                              This poem, for instance,

contains no crystal towers

                    awash in light-kissed gradations

                                        of shadow (in "fact" a wash

of luminous lavender

               up hill's dark gash

                         into woods) but you

can lick it anyway as long as

               you don't forget the split seams

               on the way in – or is that out? – just there

               where the little train

               and Candy Mountain

disappear

II.2.ii   Condensations of sidereal matter

When the earth becomes the sun
                                which way are we going? Signs
                                indicate restricted access as a condition
of egress into realms
                        of stellar events
                        done up to resemble
the corner store
                    Nothing special
just there when you need
smokes or some
sugar
        but indicating fulfillment
                                as a regular
                                image somewhere
                                just the other side
of word's work

La dolce vida
                on a bicycle
                            long slim legs
                            and a shopping
bag. Does it matter whence sweetness
                            arrives – taste of salty
                            flesh or a good deal on
                            shoes?
                                Seeing City beyond the river
of red lights occasionally
                        flashes requests for help tasks
                                            ability otherwise tied up in ceremonies
of resurrection
                    Was there ever
a wholly good deal?
The dead dog
            stinks in any case, coming

                                        apart in the fly's jaws. Is it
that same dog ranged
                    from heaven to hell, returned
                                                to bark and spin now
rendered mute?
City flickers
or winks and sudden interrogation
                                        bursts swollen tips into chill
                                        passing. Suspended invitation
                                        in a gasping salvation
                                        promises only another dawn
                                        if you're lucky
Uncertain
            but determined, City dies
                                ripped up, buried alive
                                and rises to no promise no
beat resonant with heart felt
                                contractions. Walk with me
through the valley of the shadow
                                    of capital surrounded by no thought
but more filling towers rise
                            out of earth's broken, tortured
frame to blot what's left of ancient
                                    market at the crossroads protected
by herms announce a different
                                space where *where* doesn't work
the way it used to.

Oikonomos

is a diamond and the glare of its game
                                    blinds other anticipation
                                                of possible formation of care
beyond centre field.   Sun shines

from it only when eyes adapt to new
modality of eyes and registers
of nothing slip through positions
of thoughtful
purchase. The velocity of money
                              figures into the mix and flashes
applied brakes squeal
                    anomalies of spectral termination
               in intersections of cross dimensional
               obscurity
                         Oikonomos
               is a house
full of love and the arrangement
of its pieces belies the creeping
                              nightmare breeds in wreckage
                              heaped carelessly across that
glory. City wants more
                    attuned condensations
                                        of sidereal matter deposited in accounts
of common encounters
                    with unexpected forks
                                        there all along
                                                  Proliferation renews
body of solar implication
in flicker figuration's slow
swell
     Waves is a name
                    returns to demise of coherence
                    in emerged electric sapphire
                    crackled sense dances
                    on leaf edge till bobs
out into glow of morning mist
                              over smooth Bay finds it alive
and breathing

Holes in the continuum

      gape when breath turns

and City stutters out

in the midst of endless

interpretations of *empty*

     Centreless sprawls

     against this world

its name diffuse in the dawn

      not as some argument with night

but in love with endless

discriminations of passage

II.2.III ALL TINGLY IN REGINA

On the other hand
        fire of arousal
              stirs up exceptional preposition
responses to isolation
        of Shekinah in hope's return
                  from thing's nothing to tingly
intimation Regina never knew
        it had coming
        Still eking out
every possible connection from penumbra's
              startling conventions, City
              verges
              on potential extension
        beyond real estate
        into thought
        rock has of shattered
        seasons and duration
              Endurance is often
enough to realize
        moon's commotion
        vague categories
            of shadow

              Tingly makes
no excuses, nor untoward
        gestures possibly construed
as another register
        But the containment
            of tingly proceeds
            in further formations
of concrete boxes

Abstract boxes work
                                        too, provided blinkers continue
limit of horizon's subtraction
                            to current concoction's
                            ingredient list

Slipping and sliding leave Regina
                                        confused as to anatomical
                                        configurations
                                        as specified in old-time rhetorics
                                                                It sure
feels good, but intensive
                            development leaves streets
                            with nothing
to hang their passage on, and other
                            elucidations mapped
                            with meticulous
                            attention face
transactions to the contrary

                    Then just a quickie winds up
                    confronting errors
                    of pagination with a whoop
                                                of anticipation other restraints
couldn't quite excite, though Regina
                                    never doubted climax
would support vulgar missteps
                        as a condition of salvation

Wringing every possible
                        drop of meaning
                        from its limp
                                    figure may be no more

                                        possible
than leaving City

                    satisfied after unexpected
                    assignation
                                post lunch, but hell,
                                it's worth
                                        a try knowing fate
                                        of the western
                                                world hangs in oblique
                                                reference to economic
salvation with
            or without alien insertions
                                    as a regulating function meant
to keep tingly in a place
                        Regina dreams
                        moments flirtations
of light's play
in its stony face

II.2.IV FLIRTATIONS OF LIGHT

Rocks
     scattered, broken on its wheel
                    warming to sun's wash
across their face is
as enlightened
       as it gets
          They swell
          hum
          in stone-specific key
for ages

      City hears it
          in crushed bones and up
                  through layers of accumulated
death
     Does it buzz?
        Is it
          a beat in angel-thrummed
          bridge wire? Morning blushes
          bursting in another
          direction toward earth
          thrill, opening chosen in midst
                  of each habit
Snow
     drops first,
        then tulips, then
            riot of shape and hew
            petal-specific, fragrance passes
                  as reality once calculable
            illusions are left in the dust
            of City's dream of dawn's
kiss
     How romantic is that, though
             questions remain – where's

are, who's here, what's

                we?

Getting to the arena on time

                  for example. And as Jack said

                  the Air Force Academy

                          Digest

that

    Disposing of intrusions

                of uncomfortable disposition

may obscure the question

                but it lingers in moonlight's foreshadowing

new nights in which night

                disappears

                    discontinuous

shadow discrimination, leaves

                day loose among its bearings bringing

                down the house of alternate

                hands in a clamour of crashing

                vanities of time and space

Whisper

      of water and stone is neither

                  name nor

outcome, but that doesn't mean

                it can't be heard in time between

time's tapping out unlikely

              licks

              Sheer vibratory overload

hums trajectories – trajections, really

                story's arc, costly delusion

                economies

              this *together* has brought

into law

      of horizon's subtraction

The law
          of horizon's subtraction doesn't
                              hum, more of a drone, sound
          of leaden with gratuitous
                    overtones to lend
                              a blush to semblance
of alive
          The Air Force
          Academy remains the joker
                              ubiquitous sign of not just limit
but eventual embrace necessary
                    to resuscitation of transparent
medium as a vehicle for open
                    horizons to possible reach
into edge
          Beyond is another
          matter displacing misleading
          metaphors but refusing to budge
                              from top of the sentence
                              still promising a period
                                        It's all
so clear until City
                    enters through back
                              door resembles nothing
so much as familiar
                    turn of phrase

What is the colour
                    of stars and what happened to terraces
as determinants of urban splendour
                              render a new encounter
with question of remains
                    clinging to flirtation which assumes
an aura of uneasy
                    sanctity

Then the Air Force
                              Academy glows well beyond
                                                  antithetical absence and hums
a few bars of
                    off we go
                    into the wild blue yonder
                                        before admonishing
                                        bound earth
                                                  fantasies to give it up
                                                                      Dictation
is another name for that as it
                              leaves Yankee rock piles
trying to catch wheels spinning
                              madly down the road and reeling
from metaphor to mixed
                              metaphor
                                   Giving it a name
flirts, a brush
                    of light on neck's curve or glass
                                             tower's face
and if Martians land
                    in the sentence, it's because
                                                  invasions happen and only a fool
                                                  would say no
                                                       No, not a fool
who is another name for it
                                   but a hunger
                                   artist starving for the glory
                                   of pain bound refusal buttressed hard
case anthem
                    In the Second Town
                    Martians walk down Bloor
                                             and no one thinks twice about loon
call rings the air out
                    of blue to new attention

II.2.v. HUMMING A FEW BARS

". . . every day, every instant, is the small gate through which the messiah enters."
Walter Benjamin

Speechless music larks
round corners, waiting
to mug unsuspecting adorents
a veritable theme
in the mish-mash
of moon-time
sidewalks other
worldly fragrance
If you could wish it
on sidereal remnants
it would glow
in unanticipated light
figures and the whole
thing would tingle
As long as you can
hum
a few bars, City
will pick up the beat and run with it

Coagulations are its middle
name
Or sometimes errant
issues too. The benefits of no bars
is ambiguous but tends toward
unnecessary enclosures rather than
neon alleys in San Francisco
When both
hum a few, the structural
integrity of the poem threatens
to leak, light and music grope each other

                              in licentious disregard of proper
names and open abuse of anonymous
          homonymies drives
          crazy into corners
          and cracks threaten
          to upend specs
                              fixed to syntactic clarity's
                              repeat where the bars turn
                              toward intangible but always
                              insistently held in the wall
          that's not there, too
                              No music
          puts it squarely in public
          ambiguity and indeterminable
          gestures
                    Sure, it's often disguised
                                        as a sound track to every little
                                        move, but worlds do lurk
                                        in the bars
                                                  Then humming a few
                                        takes on the mantel of City
          as Logos, but with a beat
          each hears and moves to
          without thought of wind but caught
          in branches of unrestrained
thinking anyway – deep blue
surges but also green
flicker
          Moving
toward another end, but too far
                              away to grasp the difference
                                                  an image of assembled sense
pushes toward a final
word
          There is none
          of course

                    but that never stopped breath's

                                        mysterious terminus
appears bereft of all
reference and begging
for a current site
                    Providing one

                                    hums a few bars in hope

                                            emergent areas of higher
than normal entropy can withstand

                                further development

                                            The City
                            ought to know better, but it's

                                            forgotten how, having lost
sight of the Bay and yielded to other

                            hungers assembled sense leaves
in place of lemons

                    They almost
taste like the real thing
and they're cheaper

                    Familiar tunes
are easy, but the ones you don't
know lead tonal deviations

                            into vague unease

                            with laundromats

                            and other chipped institutions

                            of public labour when knowing
better is just another case

                    of mistaken identity turns out
to be the real thing

                    Then bars may hum

                            you, in which case tune echoes

                            in variations of electric

                            blue dancing leaf edge

                                        City

                    feels it—6:04 A.M. August 15—
but it slips away taking time
                    with it
                        Landscapes enter
                            the picture as a sign
of this emptying, but forget
                    humming as a revivifying
                        prospect leaves it on other
side of the last road
                Crossing
                    from primordial
                        plenitude, a genuine hummer
                        of a state
                        if there ever was one, City
awaits itself on a corner
somewhere near
                Shadows
pool
    Light cones dot
the street
            How it got there
is a tale of affection run
                    amok, wreaking surprise
                        after surprise on unsuspecting
shoppers with its little
                    beauties abandoned in alleys
                    and broken approaches
                            Coming
to itself suggests stories of bridges
and loitering angels humming
                    almost recognizable renditions
                            of unknown tunes set
streets aglow inviting
festival of sudden recognition's
sumptuous destinies

2.II.VI   RESUSCITATION OF THE TRANSPARENT MEDIUM

"Sometimes I have believed in as many as six impossible things before breakfast . . .."
The Red Queen

Delivered or undelivered trees
fall announcing death in arboreal
agons of sub-anthro-acoustic
                                   wails

        When no one hears them
                                   he jams expansion into vacancies
of unrequited confrontation
                                   with temporal liquidity. Soaked, all the time there is roils
as usual
            It isn't the terminal
                            vocabulary with its elusive
                                            saturation – it's the question
keeps asking City to speak
to its name – a regular pain in the ass
                            Even light glints
off soaring idols signals abbreviated
emergencies
                Is it just a slip
of the tone?
                Emerson's mood shifting
                                    tonalities knotted weavescapes
                                    bursting
tips register scales past
                    measure
                        Looking down on remnant's
            roof, tattered ontic murmurs shaded
            by immense glass cages
                                    leaves it hanging in hilarious
intermissions into which flutters

spectre of past opening today's
geometry
    The sensorium
        multiplied not just here
        and there with all the sunlight, and
            come to think of it
            shadow, aplay, as in
            afoot,
                but *when*, too, which opens
whole thing into
      obscure chiaroscuro thought
           of god with dirty feet
                  Maybe

      that sun is simply mind
      returned to stones

         where it started

         vibration
         heat brings indistinguishable
partners in that dance
      City
glowing from within ignites
        Puritan ambitions even as it speaks
broken rhythms of dance, the partners
         a fallen tree and an attentive
poem, hum quietly but with no less feeling
         for direction sentence takes with each

        step chosen so quickly
        light floods the passage
            Glowing

from within is just glowing

And the rocks
do glow, even now as they did
then
Then's now
dances
too, and not just on remnant's
roof, but across the sky
depicted in glowing faces
of rock
Out of that dance
the transparent medium gasps
for breath, arrives glowing
with anticipation
of nothing further
It surges
through stories till another
kicks in rejigging essential
elements into dream of seamless
beauty
City doesn't get it
Is it stuck between a rock
and a subway dancing ecstatic
formations of transit?
The transparent
medium, having believed only
five impossible things
before breakfast tries to imagine
Scarborough but is stumped
by the impossibility of getting
around
It flips, then flops
and the whole thing screeches
to a stop
Hoping for a clearer
vision is the opiate of internally
corrupt engines everywhere

                    The Second
                              Town wonders how
                                        to move on
                                                  Denied
representation, the bars
                    all closed, it wanders City
                    looking for an angry dawn to fix
                    its melancholy up with, hoping
the union will lead to archaeologies
of new found enthusiasm
                              for eccentric selections
                                        You can't tell the effect
the end has on now
                    to register with proper
authorities
          It won't listen to your howls of protest
          once resuscitation glimpses
          further moods of civic
                    hilarity in the unimpeded vista
                              off the end of the poem

PART 3

Erasing heaven

"The name itself is the cry of naked lust."

WALTER BENJAMIN, *THE ARCADES PROJECT*

II.3.1   BETWEEN CONCLUSIONS

"Lying between the earth and the heavens, it partakes of the color of both."
Henry David Thoreau, *Walden*

A strange place to restart
                    another almost level
                                        yearning to define
angles it's not
                There's erasing itself
                pink
                plump
                crumbly
                        And then there's between
brief glimpses of stony
                        iterations
                                Between
evades   away   even
                        as it indicates directions
to the store
            leaving
limits of readability to writhe
                            in what may or
                            may not ache
in excruciating extensions
                        of meaning
                                Without
it, conclusions reek
                of excess
                        of Kantian categories
                                        Intuition
and intellect give each other
a hug while otherwise
                    hangs around corners
waiting

It's just that no
                    amount of further stops
           Read it
                    carefully, then say City
while thinking *elephant*
                    Redemption
                              of zoological uprightness
                                             hung up on questions
of transportation indicates proximity
                              to suburban distances
                                             It's a real
                    City, so the elephants
                    are real elephants,
                                   but proximity
is a problem of continually
                    getting to it without losing
                                   sight of the evidence
of domestic bliss
           in the ashes
                    The dancing king
angry and untenable in exposure's glare
                    may dictate a severe service disruption reflects
                    arrhythmic vibratory intrusion battling
                    for world dominion
diminished in arenas of popular
                    address to power distribution
beyond boardroom deals

But that's
           not erasing thought of distinct
                    and separable
                              states of encounter
with paradisiac eruptions which remain
                    the world's state
                              Tied to its
evidence is yet again another end

posing as entertainment meant

to supply adequate distraction

from the business otherwise required

to erase heaven

in the name

of a further stretch

of the imagination

If iron arcades

evaporate in voluptuary

communions with nothing

in their place

but shoddy streets

blazing toward the topmost

face of grotesque and suddenly

rowdy concoctions of cheap

dry wall's already crumbling

empire

It doesn't quite add up

but the streets are real enough

and the promise of evacuated

elephants raises the bar of real

doable levels

The end

in sight causes no end

of trouble among words

jostling for position

Stars

on the water, for instance, silent
before Thoreau's wondered
eye, or swirling
around Clark Gable's feet
as he carries Claudette Colbert
forever through the sky
toward a destiny of open
roads leave City

dreaming of elephants even

                    as nations of buffoons see

                                    nothing in the swirl

but numbers indicating

                low taxes as a gauge of god's

                              gift to individuals of great moral girth

further complicating the simple

                  image of how to go on

without heaven

          Seeing beyond

                yields a glimmer of indistinct

                              radial circulatory dreams

of a gorgeous body

         of thought threatens to break

                        out in Polly Wolly Doodle

exuberance, proving unnecessary disposition

of celestial illusions

to City's twilight glimmer

            How

to name it so that it sticks

         to that lip enunciates

boulevards lined with towering

             trees, jewelled towers leading

                        into its ordinary

                      heart

                        The Second Town

believes in the sun in a fit

         of intoxicated subtraction leaves

                        the state of things desperate

to re-establish boots on the ground

           of similar façades

                      demanding proof and unmixed

metaphors in euphoric

        assertions of subways

        to the suburbs

News of a real tree in the middle
of the kitchen comes to disrupt the corpse
flow while yielding a lively
twist to fading celestial passage
(till the Administration cites
efficiencies, progress, and easy
access for jets and issues new
regulations establishing heaven
as a mandatory requirement
for all forms of
stellar engagement

II.3.11 MERMAIDS, ARISE!

When she comes, the mountain quivers
                                    with pleasure and boxes
without topses
                are a subject
                            of exquisite scholarship
                                                The mermaids
having been declared figmentary
by The Administration, wonder
what hit them and having multiple
                            resources at their fintips
                                        consider moving to City
                                        to blend in

The mountain, meanwhile
                    having discovered itself
                    half way to heaven and recovered
                    its composure
                    wonders at how
shifting titles and revelations
yet to come leave behind
                    seismic destinies of less
                    than obvious
                    demarcation
                            Such is the way
                                        of fish and men in elusive
reflection of troubled water's
                    rippled face and a sudden
                    run-down church in near distance

                                City
disturbed by eruptions of distended
                        ectoplasmic power surges
                                        meant to level resistance
to announcements

from the Administration, refuses to go
                                        back into the box
                                        of non-speculative
                        determinations reduce elemental
                        bon mots into simple
            minded slogans
            designed to provide
            faux vegetables
            to an audience
entranced by the sight of stuff
                        glowing behind windows
                                        in the night
                                        Leaking radiance

is also an event even under
the grey dome
                For the sun to become
                                the earth, certain questions
with the stress on quest, must
                                enter the arena of passion's
attention
            Transmutation is no
                        mere sleight of hand, more
                                        of the eye as it grips down
into an earth of unexpectedly rich
                        vocabulary that leaves it
strangely speechless

The end
        of mermaids is a well-known
                                goal of reasonable Administrations dead
set on settling
once and for all
            errant spasms of imagination

                    Really
serious violations threaten
                    the definition of minstrel
                                        leading diminished expectorations
to figuratively speaking
loose ends
            After that, who knows? The next
                            stop may look palatial
                            from outside
                                        but lacking mermaids tends
                            toward tawdry points of cheap
        splayed along road's thoughtless
                        abuse of space
                        Grime
                        is not just about money but a
                        poverty of inter-dimensional feedback
                        breeding pockets of ulronic
                        loggerheads and spread
                                        of lifeless seas
They stretch
            down roads with no terminal
satisfaction beyond redemption's
                        siren call which
                        though relying on the power
                        of cliché
                            gets back to mermaids while
                            foretelling after the fact myths
of woven night
            Having been proven
                        above and beyond all reasonable
                                        limitations not to occupy
narrow sectors of space
                time stripped of nutrient
                                conjecture, they are left
to move on to more interesting
                critics and congeries

                                                    of terrors that slip the leash
of actuarial inventions, risk free
                                as far as liability
                                            goes, but not
so hot when eyes of fire
                        enter the equation throwing
                        ontic seizures around
                        objective contents and stirring up
                                                metaphysical shit
                                                with So-shu's fabled pole

            The attraction
                        of City toward elements
of questionable repute will always
                                find a way
                                in to its face
                                even pink
with the flush of sunrise
                        Mermaids
know
        reading it over and over
                                in multiple registers as they pass
from water to air, air to water
thinking
            idly of further passages
            with the mountain
                        beyond the ninth sphere

II.3.III THE DIE OF A TAKING PLACE

"But the life that begins on earth after the last day is simply human life."
Giorgio Agamben, *The Coming Community*

Baby needs a new pair
                of worlds exclaims
                                certain obvious but uncertain
digression through alleys and past
                        doorways that stand as delicious
                        indication
of coming formation and darker
                        implication
                                Not that they aren't *that*
                                door—they do open and close
but it's never the same going
                through it
                        Baby needs a new
frame and then worlds
                emerge from its head in procession
                of virtuous adumbrations declaring
                once and for all another
launch
        Ostensible security
                        of information aside, migration of several
magnitudes continues to wreak
                        disruption throughout the network's
                                far flung imposition of waiting
room's grey walls and green
metal benches
                Yes falls
                        into cringe without knowing
                                cringe

                                        Never having to read it
twice is one of the rights
                        guaranteed by contraction's gravy
                                                hallucinations
            Baby needs a new
                        tax free ecstasy zone
            and instant
                        subterranean transport through haze
                                                of oleaginous apologies
                                                and suburban deliria

of endless cheap gas and open
                        roads free of clutter non
                        automotive passage scatters heedlessly
                        in car's immaculate path
                                        This harbinger
of ruptured dimensional integrity
lodged firmly in destiny's
                        craw threatens to unleash retroactive
                                                doom vibe into the chambers
of its heart
            How to get where
            from here
            through accident of tumbling
                                bones is its *tractatus* written
in the rattle of sudden de-
                        termination
                        Meanwhile, Sultanism
                                        of the brain still hoofs it
with that guy plucked
                        from a crowd of ecstatic
                        shoppers
                                They wheel

happily through sluggish
rivers of rubber, steel,
                    red light
as far as they can see
                naming its sense in real
                            time as the small price paid
                            for admission
                            to Costco which works
out to several concurrent
                eternities of hard labour
                            Voting
for it is the only available
                option pullulating incoherencies
bring to the table
                The table's edges
                        join in the postulation ill-regulated
ambivalences are the root bred
                from declining numinous
                            examples
                                They waver
feckless but determined to hold
                those dancers to imagined
                            spread of their connection
at the boundaries of heaven
                leaving real
                        potholes all the way there
                                Awakening
brass is their other
                announcement, mystery and opacity
                            in shape etched air
                            You never
know who's coming
                around the corner
                and what
they're packing where die's modality
                shifts into cacophony of siren's

weaving night out of quitting
                             time contagions
                                        Baby needs a new
                                                  tone changing
everything even as accusations
                         of appropriation interrupt to knot
passage's charged direction
                      The rolling bones don't care
though inflections of reduced
                         visibility do spread
                                  through the aisles
                         Then the tone
becomes harsh or gentle, querulous
or certain
             The earth shifts
                    dragging heaven into a new
                                     sphere
                                Elephants appear
then leave in trucks headed
                       west
                      It's the time of slipped
moments, the age no longer
                      held to its measure, firming up
                      belief's installation in the temple
                      pushes knowledge of the country
                                     of non-where
                                    into the cold

awaiting bone's
speculative tumble

II.3.IV   CONCENTRATIONS OF HEART

"Up again, old heart."
                    Ralph Waldo Emerson, "Experience"

Encroached is an odd way
                            of darkening, but you have to start
                            somewhere as contracted light
dictates and odd light never missed
                                    which misread as mind leaves
                            a charged whirl
                                        arranged diagonally to represent
                            a significant pause
                                                    On
to the heart, exhausted by appetencies
                                of interrupted exchanges
                                                    Where's
the restroom is often the first
                                encounter with its rambunctious
                            discount
                                        Another day another
                                                    sublated sale leaves you
agape at the sheer
                    evasive agon of daily
                                obliteration
                                        Where the Second
Town lurks cracks the heart
                            into countless pieces which glitter
                            with stellar implications
in the stream of our
                    crossing
                        Stars swirl
                        flash distances of light
                                            alive in the spark of its
                            wink

                                                   A real barn burner

inflaming the heart
                    with thought of a mind
                                            on fire
                                It's not even
                                                intrepid but finally just

willing, that again, now
                        up and looking awfully like
                                                    a hero if you can shake
                                                    armour and accumulated junk
                                                    that goes with it and think – no
                                                    not that
                                                    just get

up again
        without narcotizing stuff's
                                    allure, abandonment
turned into iconic desuetude
                            in telluric outbursts leave useless
as a measure of value untouched
                                by exile
                                        Recollection of an unrecorded
journey is the stuff
                    of history as the heart has come
                                                    to suspect in compositions
of exile configured as Yorkdale's eternal
traffic cramp, the death
of circulation
                A nadir, perhaps
                                though City is inclined
                                toward less elevated
                                geography of steady
                                                    illumination casts it as a kind
                of temple in morning's splendid light
                                            but ravaged for parts

                              and left to drift into velocity

of coincidence and constellations
                              of coronary insurrection
                                             against non-sensuous compulsory
tourism

              Name your poison
              captures nuances of mythic
              dance plays out in accretions
              of density till bump we're up
                                    against it and no way out
                                    but to think the immense
                                    space in the heart
                                             of an atom as reminder
                                             of fading but insistent pulsation's
                                             rich splash and what precedes
it
   Anyway, the heart rings
                       with sympathetic tremolos
                                       of contracted release, surge's
signature as in up
                again till City, saturated
                              with morning transits
                              some star
into less nebulous concentration
                       and equality of subtle components'
                                             aspect of its vital logic gathered
in intractable clods
beneath the feet
of travellers
          while oligarchs
                       sweat in the haze
emitted by defense
          of their holdings

Their holdings

threaten to come apart

and return to the knowledge

of the three Towns but an expense

of spirit leaves only

death of the oceans

Impossibly

brutal, the blunt rapture

standardized in precise passage

of clock hands and consequent

botox alterations of the *mysterium*

into smooth, immutable

frozen measures of duplicitous

path's exact click

Up again

is the spell of its return

in a heartbeat to the feast

of earth's procession coming

forth in burst and stutter

Dawning

City is the one that knows

how to go on when the end

is close and terror of beginning

again wanders dark streets

mouthing the moon's

forgotten names

II.3.v THE CONVEX SURFACE OF THE NINTH SPHERE

"I see Doctor Jazz in all my dreams
When I'm in trouble bounds are mixed
He's the guy who gets me fixed . . ."
    Jelly Roll Morton

The stakes float on a surface
                perilously unanticipated
                by methods
                      of intense information extraction
                      Cages
of extrapolated boundaries
                yield to spaces
                      of at least the sixth if certain leeway
            is admitted as attending
to imaginative
          stretches
            So the ninth
                if you can find your way
there is no
simple extension
          more like a sky
              inside out
            What a sky is echoes
with more elementary combinatory
                exquisites, a material form
                      of mind's movement among common
            iterations of wonder
                and trajectories any
moment condenses in bustle
          of ordinary logs
            on the fire

                                        Licking is then
both a time
rupture and a new
                    manifestation of elephants
                                    on the move through godded
extents of maple, oak, chestnut
                        toward paradise, or at least
                                            California, all green and golden

in bankrupt air

It beats
Scarborough
and other rapidly
transiting breaches
                with what god
                        gave us, as they say when
                                        the ninth sphere tending
                                        toward a kind of excitement
                        normally reserved for serious
                interdimensional fissures
gets grave about the lack
                of eye contact
                            Sincerely cubed
seems like a good idea
                but *chronos* has split
                            and City reels in the face
of that cruelty
                Abandoned to merely
                        rude and ignorant with no further
                        interdimensional break
                        through to pump up
    the *tremendum* as an over
                    riding frequency adjustment

                                                            sucks City into democracy's
worst nightmare

The ninth sphere
                looks on stunned
                                by eruptions of extreme encounters with part
and parcel of northern landscape's
                                voice
                        meant to seal the deal
                                        of vaguely recalled imperial outposts
before the chorus of hallelujahs
                        turns the thing upside down
                                                Ruptured
                planes, indeed
                        Yet old plans
for Parisian boulevards
                still animate boxes of distinct
                                        urban dream time vibrations
just outside the bounds
                of acceptable behaviour
                                City throbs
                                        with implicit sense of end
                                        less openings into sphere
                                        after sphere of elephants strolling
down Kingston Road in full
                knowledge boundaries
                                may reseal at any moment
but not giving a hoot since
                they have been welcomed
                                        into the folds of its
                                lucky irresolution
                                                The concave
surface is not so fortunate
                in its necessity but you can't
                                escape it even as yearning

for clear resolutions of City's
                              dream passage
                              through relational densities
                              not so much
determined as accidentally
stumbling into focus keeps
                              popping up

                              Without it is a rock
pile where Yankee ghosts
                    have been known to settle in
                                        respect to hard rejection
and a particular twist
                    of imagination into a kind
                                        of knot
                                        The stories that stop
thinking
don't get there
because there
stops believing
in them
          Dr. Jazz
                    taking shape in a new thinking
                    of *fix* has been known to make rocks
                                        dance
                                        Mixed bounds standing
in for blues is a thought to hold as he
                    names trajectories and ruptures worthy
                    of *the cry of naked lust*

II.3.VI   AXIAL ORDINATION: THE CALCULATION OF SUBLATION

"Just near this phase transition, just at the edge of chaos, the most
complex behavior can occur – orderly enough to ensure stability, yet full
of flexibility and surprise."
                    Stuart Kauffman

Ordinarily you wouldn't think
                                        axial beyond common
                                        specificity
of rotational anchorage and large
                        ice surface
                        but that's how aeonic
                                        contraction crumples the aspect
when you're not looking
                    leaving
sublation flopping on the deck
                    of the seventh sphere wondering
                    how it got there
                                    Phase modulation
too
    Syntactical opening leaves
                        cosmic phantasy to devices
                                        otherwise known to authorities
                        as dangerous offenders
                        of the status quo disguised
                                        as upside down flower
The uproar
            resembles elephant trumpet
                            resounding through narrow
street for the first time
                Knowing
nothing is ever lost to tangled sky
                    lacery of winter
                    leaves window on window
                                    speculating

as to *when*'s claim to non-rotational
                                ordination
                                        Ordinarily
it wouldn't be a problem but
                        the loom enters and rearranges room's
directive, introducing religious
                        discipline in connection with
primordial eruption's linked
                        beginning
                                Woven threads
                                        lead neither in nor out but hold
bits of broken light along radial spread
                                of its hunt
                                Axes wobble
as we have known for some
                        time so now the problem
                                        of tracking City's modulation
involves shifting stars
To be
        or not to mill around is not
                        a question currently at stake
                                                as various construction
                                                sites where looms
                                                tend toward
compositions of monotonal
                        utility and guaranteed
                                                understanding the first time
                                                through—no re-reading
                                                required
                                                        It's just that the orders
of sense spreading from each
                        word tend to over
                                        lap creating amplified wave

patterns entangled with incoming

           images promising story of mystery

                  journey so that the whole

fabric yielded loom tangled

        thing just stops and there's time

             to visit

             Each new degree for lack

of a better word increases equally

        whole threat, obliterating even

        shadows of its commission

             But that's

the breaks,

that's the Administration's

        revenge for forgetting it never

            ceased regulating stacked ranks

            of voluntary enumeration in deep glow

            of shop window

               City

            awakes to a stranger's smile

in a café, but knowing that ain't

        the half of it

          What's beyond any edge

lives next door

    Or not

    The danger

known in other axial orientations

        by names fuelled with shadow

            is a fact though it's often

lost to sociology

     The order of its

        threat breaks the heart

     in two pieces rattle around

        a racket invented to obscure

     tellurian eruptions through sleight

        to maintain current level

of visibility

Strangers everywhere
              disturb tranquil illusions with further
                                duplicitous fermentation

                                          After all
even if outside is in, it's still
                    outside if you count proximity
as an ounce of technique
                    in exchange for shrouded
aspect's raid on consensus

The Second Town picks up the tempo
                              realizing City is stunned
          by spring as it writes out bits
                              of sky in folios and extraordinary
          openings thrust through icy mud's
                              resistant embrace into zone
of anarchy and ordinary
                    transformation of rotational
anchorage into end time's
                    currency exchange, petal like
                    hesitancy
                    hard against cold light

BOOK THREE

Uproar

In the third Town the man
shall have arisen, he shall have concluded
any use of reason, the Dialogue
will have re-begun. The earth
shall have preceded love. The sun
shall have given back its deadly
rays, there shall be no longer any
need to be so careful. The third Town
shall have revealed
itself.

CHARLES OLSON, "POEM 143. THE FESTIVAL ASPECT"

PART 1

Hot tacos cold beer

"And was Jerusalem builded here among these dark Satanic mills?"

WILLIAM BLAKE, *MILTON*

"the answer:

the glass perfectly dark, or

burning in pieces."

ROBIN BLASER, "HONESTAS"

III.1.1 WITH GUACAMOLE

The possible ghost world behind the green
island disappears in mist
north
    Having earned it
             extends ranges
             of reference beyond highway
             or breaks it in two, then forgets
ascension as accomplished
righteousness
        You'll know it
when you see it—an outset so blank
and terrifying, recklessly
addressed to disfigured
recipients, it can only mutter
            in darkness
            Behind the western sun
is lost in the single image left
            after its death, the end
of the ride

Behind the sun
knowing in pieces
is enough to satisfy demand
           for answers
             As if light
hadn't already taught us
       Then
guacamole means a kind of grace
a kind of flesh, a layer
of soft, green *pulchritudo*
to quote Pico though he threw in
            voluptas not to mention *amor*
            and he wasn't thinking of tacos

though that doesn't matter since tacos
are a perfection, on the street
or in other venues of indistinct
equilibrium
                    Transitory, true
                              but Pico would probably get over that
                              given the wedding
                              of flavours and texture, guac
                              oozing into implications
                              and further cracks
                              in the grind of the Administration's
punctilious arrangement of *amor*
designed for banners at blowout
                                        weekend sales events
                                                  Walking
                              through that adamantine
                              mall, ersatz voluptuary
                              contractual telos mirage
                              displayed in pulchritudinous
                              plain old must have tickle
                              you there by the short hairs
                              arrangements is not
a sign but an actual passage
through real collapse
                    But then
it doesn't look like you think
it will

It never does

The Third Town
isolate, is nothing: behind
the sun is the sun
                    become the earth
                    in the sky

                    The Third Town
thinks justice is pulchritude and finds it
in City's bones
                    Guacamole is the name
it brings to the wedding
when years later it shows up
to complicate the picture
with ramped up street
                    depth and shoulder to shoulder
                                        jostle, together beginning
                                        here

Political commentary suggests
a breakdown in City's
sanitation services has extended
into other modes of lingual
condensation wreaking havoc
with the uproar
                    Pulchritude
                    refusing to leave, seeks shelter
                    in public opinion's court
                    but is driven to the edge
                    of town, dumped in antiquated
                                        residues of meaning, and left
                                        shivering by the side of the road

The question of firmament remains
relevant to the outcome
                    If the lotus grows
                    downward, where is the flower
and what support are we
talking about?
                    The end
                    of reason? Conversation is the face
                    of the outcome's deferred
                    agreement, so at least, then, stones
                    dug up with broken nails

                    laid level in the gouge, ascension's
                    foundation in conversation's
                    difficult to pin down
                                        subject
                                        Think *dying throes*
                                        of tiny black holes and imagine the return
                                        of faeries
City is jubilant
              Former mayors
mayors and would be
mayors gather in squares
claiming to solve its problems
                          Recorded
elephants trumpet in streets festooned
with lotus banners and metaphorical
references to the glory
of guacamole

But the Third Town
feeling hinky
hangs back, recalling rumours
of a green island and wonders if it
too is behind the western sun

                    The ghost world
                    isn't dead. The outset
                    staggers
                          If it's visible, in what
                    register is always at stake
                    and those who want to hold it
                    to the *fact* are not averse to force
                    of reason as a means of overpowering
                    fractious residue of pulchritude
                    not to mention voluptuous haunches
                    and amorous intent

What's the name
of the guy who sang the beat
                        goes on?
Yet there it is, and guacamole
oozing too, and so on
a culmination
fit for initial dispositions
                        of love's archi-spatialities

III.1.II   Untoward festivities

"The heart in the darkness of City sings
It answers the song of the source, the sun."
Robert Duncan, *Heavenly City, Earthly City*

Maybe it's because too early
is not toward enough
to qualify
for festivals much less
festivities
though its mystery
appears as a bird
which City incorporates
in lurid emblems and signs
of aspiration
But too early
is just a slip of a thing
not yet aware of what's
to come
in all its festival aspect
Arian heresy
be damned the Three Towns
mutter, infinitely restless and caught
in thump's fascination
and immediate ranges
of Amor arriving from adjacent
accidents to complicate
interconnected incursions and ramp
up chaos to a level sufficient
to incubate a dancing
star
The uproar spreads as
transitory certainty rises
from beneath
where it lay
all along

                    Uproar is the noise
countless conversations rising
in crescendo's raucous
blended sound seemingly
coherent though unsettled finally
yield in the unresolved
sentence
            Then Astaire
                        slips in, a prophet of space
of drifting connotations
and endlessly leaky referents

You want festive?

The dance proceeds through adamantine
resistances leaving swing
                        time the logical conclusion
                                    Space
between the Three Towns
or not
        determines lost ranges
of transmission, the messages
reaching beyond themselves
to indicate proliferation
of vibratory sources and ranges
of together
                Strangers
everywhere
            And flourishing
                        zones fleeting circumscriptions
written round with secret forays
                        into declarations
of ecstasy

In this scheme *things*
brings to disposition
of eyes' range
                        Astaire
                              takes to the sky
as if born there, usurped
                              star leaking into the dust
of our hood, that *gloire*
of an earlier desire in alleys
of untoward digression and yapping
                                    The festival aspect
eyes the Third Town, searching
for antecedents in dingier
                        recesses
                              and the wreckage
of mangled children
                        There is no end
to its talk of further egress
into boulevards of elegant
design
            Maybe they just feel
untoward because the hospital
is always in flames, mingling
smoke with the screams
                        of the wounded
                              The rhythms
of that haunch roil
in over darkening Bay
flooding passages
with black skies' crack
                        Then the festival aspect
recalls gathering swell unfolding
temporary curvature
on water's glass
                  Elephants still stagger
home from the party
collapsing in heaps
of ecstatic haunch

But the Third Town is tenuous
though it knows Fred's
residual meaning
answers outset's cry

Sometimes it seems impossible
to get there from here
mixed prepositions in

by toward above a maze
of sign posts indicate
interdimensional party around
the next corner
where residual meaning
intersects imaginary
being's *raison d'être*
In that sketchy neighbourhood
festival is another name
for *now* though aspect opens it
to clouds out of the northwest

The earth glows

Words do that, dragging
the Renaissance into direction's
inclination toward unruly
formats
Glow sneaks in through rents
in vapour's chiaroscuro mirage
of a manifest horizon

Strangers everywhere, each
with a riddle
Fred Astaire dances
upside down proving the state
of festivities is piratical
even as untoward drifts toward
real doozies

III.1.III PHARONIC MENTALITY

"First of all, there would have to be an outside."
Philippe Lacoue-Labarthe, *The Subject of Philosophy*

Rhymes with moronic the First
Town yells out the window
at passing objects, given propensity
to oversimplify situations
of more than regional reach
      especially if the region
is bathed in sunlight
and May's popping
    Demonic
unification leaves it
    bumping
      around there,
    the sun a distant object
        the solution
a curve in configuration
    space
    Popping is not
quite right, but burgeoning
drags in armorial digressions
distract City from the ruined
interior of memory's play
    When the mystery
    of three becomes one
    the name changes
rejecting light off the facets
of its face
    Locked into unforgiving
      images of roses
      as singular complacencies is still
      a sign waiting to come

                                    apart in specificities of silver
                                    birch against steel blue
                                    restlessness
                                              Creations
of the world lie there beside
you, a surprise, splendent
                        unaccountable order
                        of increase
in mere accumulation
of vocabulary
                  The street
opens, tree lined cathedral
corridor into further
branching and implication
of tenebrous satisfaction
in evening's fading heat
                        Pharonic
implies a porch greeting
the street in quiet arrangements
of interest and attention
                        Then City rises – not
                        so much from dust
                        as of it –
                              dust art to dust art
and Pharonic returnest
to pulchritudinous dispositions
of meaning resembling
backyard cardinal's announcement
                                    to the sky
                              It's just that the view
alters with each newly acquired
word and its possible
                        adumbration spreads
in ungainly display of festive
enthusiasm till the corner store

glows

It's there to be seen, not
a perfection of swift passage
through reasonable compositions

but open to the thought
of excessive depth
The Third Town addresses itself
to consideration of glowing

as if Pharonic
was simply a matter of attention
to where it leads into other
compositions of visibility

The firmament
shudders but refuses to abandon
scenes of invasion to men
coming to do you good

City appears
unrepentant, unfurling
petals of time, neither ascent
nor descent capable of scaling
the blur

But Pharonic for all its
bad rap in the Age of Twitter
and Rampant Duck Boys, still leads
into ancient terraces and receding rows
of pillars fading into thinking
some other order of space

Moving
in there rhymes with leaving
home, though you might not
know it to hear it

Pharonic ears
hear lotus when none is to be had

in the usual offerings, asking can there
be an end to the reign
of ends, a messenger with no other
message than the messenger
with no other message
                        The usual
                                    residues celebrate, having once
                                    again saved the world from love
                                    returned it to earth's
                                    bosom, a strange word wrested
into Calvinist euphemism's
ever ready displacement
of Pharonic juice by *1959*
                            Still
                                there it is, soft, welcoming
the curve of its allure an upside
down flower
                Leaving
                home and coming home
                are pharonically engaged in preceding
love, drifting away
                    on a tangent
                                The Third Town is nothing
                                without the three towns
                                                Pharonic mentality
is an opening the firmament
hands the sky in a gesture
signifies origami roses and tipsy
elephants
                The sky gets it and then the earth
                                                unfolds
                It's one of *those* stories
                but seeing them emerge
                                    in such vertiginous articulations
of splendour still manages to leave
imaginary being in a swoon

III.1.iv Unresolved residues of meaning

"The word of thinking is not picturesque; it is without charm."
Martin Heidegger, "Logos"

They may have salubrious scents
if lingering vibes have their way
with outsets
      Strange turns of event
mean something, though exact
determinations are rare
        The Third Town
may become one, salubrious for sure
but strange, and forever unsure
the input will stay where directed
          or wander off
          into some barely
          credible proposition, an imaginary
sea town, hardly immaculate
but still perfect in that ordinary way
of sea towns' immaterial
exchanges with mermaids and unrepentant
nostalgia for Atlantean implications
of glowing flesh
      Agglomeration
        and metastasized
        bland advance
levelling forests, eternal eruption
leaves the three Towns obliterated
in the unworld's fact
       It weighs
        a lot
         and single handedly
rids the world of mermaids, sweeping

them away with relentless
reasoned proofs and occasional
auto-de-fés made up to look
like a weenie roast on the fourth
of July
        The residue of glow
        in embers becomes
                new stories
            of unaccountable depths
and profligate festivities

Facts waver and resolution
extends otherwise clarity
into vision of drunk
elephants staggering home
collapsing in piles of voluptuous
haunch
        Party time in the land
        of strangers
            The Third Town
            shows up to lend a hand, freed
            from fixation, game for bending rules
into origami roses reeking
of salubrious scents return
through fragrant residues and shameless
circularity, dragging various
non-sequiturs and red herrings
with them, to take it
            to heart, to the beginning
            even
as it's lost in surprising
maze imaginary being
leaves in its wake

                    Rescue involves
                                    ditching the car and climbing
                                    under fences though the idea
of it soon disappears
                    Rescue
                    from what?
                                    The tangled streets
and gangs of unruly prepositions?

Any other ease of access
would suffer equal obfuscation, Avenue
Road beginning to waver
in a haze of redundancy and the pressure
the Third Town brings
to the equation
                        Where does the poem end
City begin?
            Are words ready
for prime time?
                The arrow
goes straight to the heart
of matter and the shattered fact
yields lover's kiss
on morning street or the blare
of horns extend the story
into dancing stars and the difference
that three makes
                    Materially
                    speaking, City clamours
                    for more guacamole knowing
                    full well authorized substitutes
                    can only make matters less
fragrant

But the stars are uncompromisingly

mental

insist on forms of intricate

relation

Behind the western sun looms
a warp in every possible outcome
spreads each new thought
through unsure extensions of summer's
evening shadows

Stories of glory
seem to coalesce swirling
fog around faint outline
of a City yearning to be

a firmament

You can almost see it

if you squint into the sun, a fact well
past thought, a sudden
silver birch

refusing to yield, just there
where sky turns
beyond awash
in light

The Third Town struck
with wonder at the First Town's
mundus and residue's
daily space opens in fact's
heart to festive

III.1.v   Rhythms of the haunch

The shifting weight of grace beyond codes
of judgment moans
                                yes
                                        as if it were obvious
to any uproarious festivity
contained in the sheer thump
it brings to Second Town's
daily fare
                Flowering earth thumps
                too, the roots elsewhere, H.D.'s
                reddest rose unfolding
                                        in indignity *here* brings
to flesh's passage

Guacamole lingers
                        at the edge of reciprocal
                        action behind the sun
                        but harbours hard pieces
                        of oscillation which become
                                                its name, Ganesh
perhaps
        passing through trees.

Now he has come here, too
                                left the zoo to devices arranged
                                like letters in humane
                                calcifications of boxed
                                thought
The eros
that divides the three Towns
is a frequency modulation
                                and the elephant that walks
                                through trees still knows
                                the sway of time's strange moves

                                        announced in bird throat
                                        or sudden green thrust
                                        through asphalt
                                                    City trembles
at the thought, unsure what
matter of fact means
softly and with fate weighing
it here, its green island out of
smooth, unbroken water
into swing time
                        Swing time eludes corn
                        with Africa's unerring
                        thump as waves carry
                                        sunlight over clarity of aqueous
proposition's rise
and fall, always somewhere
else, a quiet uproar

Coming apart swings
                        eliciting dialects of flesh
                        demand room to stretch
                                                beyond
                                                contraction's lump

Opening dialects
of flesh to further consideration
seems appropriate
seems true to blue
                        green dance defines edge
                        of things
                                        even in City's heart where it
has been known to leave
whole civilizations smouldering
                                in its wake

Awakening heaves
grace of butterfly wings
in evening light

The first word sounds
like that, full of lyric
noise but game in spite
of time's uses' shrivelled
outcomes
        Sucked dry but still
                thumping
              Rhythm varies
as seasons' passages
within clinging fabric
of real attention, undetached and
unconcerned with civilization's
                discontents
It's not exactly promise
though the land of its
implication is always there,
lush, prodigious, impossible
beneath the loomed fabric
of antagonisms and atrocities
              of dubious heave

If it's all dance, how
does it get so bloody?
          How
does the garden become hell?

The Third Town wonders
what Nietzsche would do
and if any pirate utopias
are nearby
        while nearly
overcome by din

of spreading combat discourse
of reasoned drowning
out querulous attempts
to talk to the crowd gathered
to enforce justice on anyone
out of line with current
logic order of blame

It turns so quickly, beat
                    lost, rhythm faltering
into four four predictions of endless
                              brutal repetition

The *first war*'s nocturnal
formulations of stellar exuberance
are lost to gun and barrage
                    a misunderstanding
                    of *strife* into collapsed
word rubble, projective disposition's
archi-spatiality shift into democracies
of death
              City burns, smoke rising
in illegible hieroglyphs
immediately translated
into goads toward more separate
mumbling in corners

Still swaying weight of haunches
along threshold of finitude
swings come hell
or no water
                    clinging strangeness
knowing opening
                    the three
Towns marshal to the end
of facts past that
                    block face

II.2.VI   Sustaining imaginary being

Getting into it is not without moments
of terror
      alone
the poem lurking
            in some dark corner,
          you not knowing
what it's capable of

          You or it
           especially in the light of further
implications of diversified rhythms
and sudden uproar
transforms the proletariat
into pirates
        Avast heaving, comrades,
        our utopia was here
              all along – small enclaves
of imaginary being requiring
little sustenance
most of it thieved
from surrounding poems – guacamole
                elephants
                   global warming
                     coyotes

Imaginary being swings
into action in the nick
        of time

Standing there, waiting
for the poem to leap
from behind the door to another
state of vibratory reception
while maintaining your balance

and equanimity is a sign of adamantine
fracture
                    The Three Towns quiver
in anticipation
                        of the evaporation
of *some thing* in the scrutiny
substance of relation brings
to the table of conversations

                                No one
can see it all, but knowing
fruit of expenditure
in wild connotations
sustains exchange and passage
through trees and various
talking points into uproarious
irresolution conversant
with developments
between words
                        Infinite
                            qualification is then possible
imaginary being oozing
across poems breaking every
rule and generally
                        heading into untoward
                        festivities
spill over the edge leaving
an ontological mess

                    City comes
to a standstill on the surface
of another folding of depths up
                                rising in thought
of island stillness on dark
measures of middle

                          The firmament
ain't what it used to be, or they
just don't make firmaments
like they once did
                          is the answer
                     that keeps on giving
                                   A sky is still a sky
as time goes by
but a firmament
is hard to come by

                     Imaginary being
thinks city without one
and then regrets it
                     Dark
satanic mills ain't the half
of it
      Pillars into glass
      bank towers, colonnades
      into transit numbers
                          Imaginary being
                          is restrained
                          in a euphemism
on Queen St. till experts judge
it's in touch with real
                          facts and capable
                          of ideological
analysis
          The uproar recedes, lost
to traffic noise and the crash
                               of another window spewed
                               onto the street from Shangri-La
                               in gesture even contempt
finds stunning

The windows are like
                                similes
                                              and the business
they expose to the light
of comparison
                                is shoddy as the loss of specific
singular knowledge means
                                              city is doomed to hell
equivalence erects in souls
of its captives impressed
into service of factual assault

                                The Third Town
                                wants to push off
but doesn't yet have purchase
                                              re-oriented into grip

                                Yo ho ho, it sings
and a bottle of rum
                                The poem hums
along, throws its arm
around your shoulder
and takes a long slug from the bottle
                                              as levels of reference
find themselves disheveled
                                and talk turns
to mermaids, what's buried
where

        It does begin to look
like something will happen
if only imaginary being can recall
the damned password

                    Ahoy
may do, or voluptas

                         Then snap
it opens, a revelation
of triangulation, the whole
thing beginning to firm up
in a map with no orient
                              no way up
                              so that Astaire
                              dancing on the ceiling
is the compass of reorientation
indicating end of the reign
                              of ends is just another
rolling set nestled within larger
                              and larger
every which way's
sustaining scud

PART 2

The logic of erogenous zones

"The City is peopled / with spirits, not ghosts, / O my love . . ."
H.D. "CITIES"

III.2.1   SEVERAL OCTAVES OF UNIVERSE

Stammering translation results
from overlaid condensation's
impenetrable sense of erogenous
                         logic hemmed in but raring
                  to go
                              This could be the uproar

long referred to in vague
textual dispositions
                  Pliny the Elder
comes to mind for reasons
best left to lingering harmonious
suggestion of former
                  plenitude
                              But stacked
certainly, in careful order
                        Frequencies are the answer
often resorts to last
ditch effort regulated by syntactic
progress through thought
of such arrangement
                  Down
                  over the Bay, faint peach
                  at the edge fore
                  telling gradations of glory
If this bloody sky is each
                         morning awash in the same light
then where's a bay to turn
                  for answers?
                  Precession
is a dime a dozen in these
                  ports
                              It's all there, shoulder
to shoulder beginning
                  again

It's just that each one's a real
pisser, and behind the western sun
is no place to get caught
without a story capable
of withstanding harshest

evasions

The reign of ends
having ended decides to lay
low in Mexico till the worst
blows over and think

about geo-iconography and its role
in the Third Town's orientation
toward warm nights

and surf roar

But the end is never far
even if the reign is laying low
in sunnier climes

The end of City
occurs at numerous
hard to judge points in dimensions

of unequal quiddity, although you can't
rule out simple brutality
as a perpetual rupture

In search
of a practice with is its own

myth

in a world abstracted empire
of forms disguised as the real
thing leads to reconstitution

a shack on a pond lingers
in animal otherness brought back
into the world from closed
depths of ruin's domesticated
arrangement of descending
units of matter's fact

Terminal disposition
hovers, not so much behind
the door as within
moral partiality
                    a glint
                    in the eye to hint
at firmament in tone
delusional confidence mounts

                                        against *rate of movement*
                                        of vortical narrative line for more
                                        straight forward solutions
                                        satisfactory outcomes send sleep
                                        to regions of judgment
undoes the Third Town's increments
                                            of distinction

Exhortation's railing reduces
receptive capacity of loitering
thoughts further consideration
                                        of intensification
                                        The emanative circumference of further
spaces opens musical
                        dispositions
                            Shut up and

                                        listen
                                            Look

too
        The dancing blue electric
        edge of things is only the warm
        up, dawn's luminous peach blush
        infuses
                    glass, stone, steel
                                        Then behind
the western sun looks out on all those
narratives scrambling to become
home and decides
to party

Invitations abound as other octaves
spread the word of erogenous
logic's emergence among *giant*
blows of the sport
of Intellect

        The giants sport up
        and down the scales and spaces
        where liberty approaches
        moral fulfillment
        but lyric
intensity still fails
        to show up leaving button
        down temporal control
        mechanisms in a panic fearing
erogenous logic unleashed
as a general category may include
                to plod
                    toward whatever
                    end while placing one
foot in front of the
other

III.2.II   RESTLESS DISPOSITIONS OF POTENTIAL EVENTS

"We do not yet possess ourselves."
Ralph Waldo Emerson

It does go on, will or no will
whatever that is, say, Jack's
                              intent without overpowering
                              focus but still directed
as the eye, caught
in visibility's modalities leads
to new words buzzing
with ineluctable pizzazz
                    Must be time for a check up
                    with the epistemologist
                                        Disinterested
              pleasure is an alien
                              energy disposed toward angular
increments of sky
              A little to the right
              or left leaves City reeling
              from a dearth of fundament
              in a world long known to value
              the certain price
                              Expansion is a thought so directional
as to prohibit serious consideration
though it does come apart
and the view intensifies according
to the velocity of the event
                         One
                              thing for sure, the Empire
                              of forms is never far
                              away, and clever rhymes are just
                              its stamp
                                   Say to be

> *and* not to be is the question
> and also the answer

and so closes in on a tale
of the Three Towns' destiny's
completely moral transfiguration
within Ulronic rights distribution's
perennial clampdown

> City
> is a big place and interested
> vectors intersecting beyond
> fields of attention
> bear figures of surprising
> resonance and vibratory
> amplification, almost as if
> other where's leak
> into dark, slumberous bliss
> was enough

Enough means

> let's get it on has reached its

> inevitable encounter with broken

> hearted issue's curtailed
> dénouement so that it's never
> enough, at least not before enough
> has reached escape velocity
> plod may or may not
> include in deliberations
> the blows of intellect foretold
> in poems of splendid intent

The Third Town knows
it well, knows strange texture
fact becomes in light
of sport

> knows disposition's

                              position to be a matter
of unprecedented windows
and further interlude extending
into any firmaments longing
for an end of sky

                      It does go on
a wonder of all that intricate
passage only City knows
adds up beyond
map's intersection with Jurupa
and Streeter to slip
into registers of western
solar
          vistas
                    Their ordinary
                    irregular eruptions of electric
                    blue dancing edges
                    settle into knowledge trees store
                    against rising and falling
                    ebb and flow of light's wobble
                    in rock's pitch through reaches
                    interminable
                              That City just won't quit
                              even if public words
                              have been stacked
                              and numbered
                              in large facilities
                              with easy access
                              to points of distribution
                              across grid weave vanities
                              of time and space redisposed

                                        in dreams of deterred hate
                                        as if deterrence could
                                        turn democracy
                                        into once upon a time's
                                        recurring desire
                                        for laminar
                                        field resolution's
                                        final stasis

The Second Town
howls with laughter
thinking of dominion's perpetual warfare
with *giant blows of intellect's sport*
and the conquest
of hate
through appropriate
linguistic output codes

                    Small local bursts
                    of narrow satisfaction may
                    alleviate guilt's hold on anxious
                    finitude's lust for error's end

                                        while millennial
                                        interference renders *poesis*

at the limit as founding
City's founding of
the edge of *poesis* disposing
event through boulevards
and alleys restless
              founding

III.2.III   ANOTHER NICE GESTURE OF EPIPHANY
for Curtis

"It just breaks my heart that she was taken from us like that," she
said of her Yorkie, snatched by a coyote while relieving itself in the
family's backyard. "It's just not how it should be in City."
Reported in the *Toronto Star*

It is not the beginning anymore
though the beginning always
knows the designation
may change once the onset leaves
registers of intent
in the uproar
        The Third Town
        now here, or at least close
        enough to know the difference
        of increments
        ferments

Firmaments
        are overrated when the whole thing
        comes down to a quarter
                of an inch this way
                or that

Look at this
        form that is never
        more nor less than
        a grace of increments and a line
                of immaculate inquiry leading
to adventures time never
saw coming

                    Every day begins
                                        before, finishes after
            moment awakens to
            trajections increments
            of surprise
                                City is stunned
        by the view *behind* offers
        wants to bathe
                        in light if only light
        is willing
                It comes down
                                    to beginning no longer
                                    being down but being
                                    here

                                    Followed of course
                                    by functionaries'
                                    days of wine and
                                    rancorous bozos distilled
                                    mania fade into token
                                    adjustments that fail incremental
                                    disposition's possible jump
                                    into dimensional expansion dragging
                                    the Third Town into untenable
                                    if not downright obscene
                                    positions in various
                                    stellar arrays

City endures material
analogy's death grip
on the throat of whatever
song tries
to rise but turns
into metaphorical displays
of well-mannered, often
clever vectors leave

market atwitter with potential
prize winning affirmations
of success
        Somewhere to the north
                migration grinds
                to a halt and a new
                epiphany blooms
                        If you call it unspeakable

are implications bearable
            or does asphalt sock
                    hold against subterranean
pressures looking
for an opening?
        Avoiding easy departures
                into neverland's perfect arrangemnent
                of plastic pirates and mermaids
                is the first order
                      But real

fisherman have been known
to violate extreme prodigality
and leave it bleeding
            on the pool table

The unspeakable girl
drowns in shadow till the Third Town
steps in when an enormous blow
opens its prospects
            to vista's intricately misted
            suggestions of City's
            streets in February's steel
            morning, with just a hint
            of heaven
                Coyote
                  wanders the edge

of manifold hungers, in
and out of light, knows
                              a tasty bite
when it sees one
                    Too many corresponding
                    registers of story leave
                    City staggering but its measure
                    was never meant to equal
                    coyote's stochastic indication
                    of myth eruption
                    in the backyard
                                        The unspeakable girl
is there too, and Behind
the Western Sun who has yet
                              to utter the name of its
                              arrival as a vector field
                              into the lingering vapours
                              of morning

They can no longer
keep track of what hasn't
happened to conspicuous
manifestation's resistance
to comfort zone's desperate
                              exclusions
                                        Coyote
                                        loves that
                                              Snacks prance
                                              in well-lit, manicured
                                              arenas of slaughter

The Third Town
looks on as flows begin
to emerge from uproar's
                              muttering merciless interference
                              patterns play across

face of City's entangled
ifs and bursts
                of incremental enthusiasm
for wild incursions
into its simple heart

III.2.IV ALEATORY INDICES OF THE REAL

"The mind can go forth to the End of the World from any point of departure . . ."
John Clarke

As a matter of fact, shifting
                              tonalities remain beneath or now
                              actually part of the uproar, even
as fact dances, electric blue
                              flashing edge of its surprising
                              buzz, its dive
                                        into a world
of entangled domains
                    Care comes
                    into it canceled
                    though clings
to aspirations of mundane
                         exuberance that just won't
                         quit rewriting the beginning

Bones
      buried
            within City's furious
            rush pave passages into
            delirium of firmament
            scream
                    Forgetting their anguish
leaves the three Towns adrift
with no title, no clear spread
of administered meaning
organized into domestic
                        revelation
                              Formerly substantial
                              arrangements of moments
                              crude and thuggish

extrapolations writhe

beneath uncertainty's thumb

leaving permanent excised
from arctic iris's purple
announcement holds the dark
to measures of appropriate
anticipation

Does it matter

what it's called?

Does the next one

care?

The Third Town tries

to reassure City its indices
are up to date and its poem

progresses

though City is in doubt, an area
just off the main strip, sensing
dawn's hesitation in the flicker
of care around real aleatory
designations as a sign
of unlikely event's origin keeps

restarting in improbable

but indispensable dispositions

of clarity's shards

Leaving City and its language

to languish in orphaned
anguish, the poem is free

to rhyme its own terms
reassemble connections
into indexical, overlapping

tunnels, not through
as there is just *between*'s
inside

out
　　Now we are getting somewhere
　　the Third Town mutters, aiming
　　for positive in the face
　　of the poem's intransigence
　　ambivalence and paralytic

　　　　　　　　　　　　　redundancy

　　　　　　　　　　　　　　　When the Concubines
　　　　of the Illumnati return
　　　　(before having left)

　　　　　　　　　　　　laughing at tales of an earth
　　　　　　　　　　　　before love, the apparatus
　　　　　　　　　　　　shudders at further adamantine

revelations, but then talk turns
to Literature and hope

　　　　　　　　　　fades

　　　　　　　　Centralities of provenance
　　　　　　　　ignore Earth before love

though coyotes
from other poems have long known
advantages of its westward

　　　　　　　　　　　extension and erogenous
　　　　　　　　　　　logic

　　　　　　　　Before love
　　　　earth vibrates
　　　　　　　they howl

　　　　　　　　　　　moon quivers

　　　　Waves, electric blue return to dance
　　　　unriven to spherical broadcasts
　　　　of galactic *terrain vague* echoes
　　　　elicit alternate turns into sketchy
　　　　doorways

It throbs

> beyond traffic pulse, erupts
> into multiple scales materializing
> backyard display of ecstatic
> perception's strange
> popping and pushing

> > up and out

> > > > The Third Town emerges

into uproar's unfinished
business, the elephants long

> > gone, the western sun
> > adrift in a sky of barely
> > recalled extensions

> > Story

nestled in the Third Town's arms
quietly expands
the thought of tree, recovering
contact long

> lost to non-aleatory

> > calculations
> > of board feet

> > then wobbles
> > and wanders into exquisite

> > > mazed

implications of honey and light
and liquefaction of bees, now

> > falling under onslaught
> > of yet another profitable
> > short cut leaves earth

> > > beneath City
> > > drenched with death

History is its name
looking like a bad
morning after blurred days
of rotgut and nicotine

No hermetic definition here
just doom's
certainty inundating
hope of honey

though
labyrinthine necessity's
doubled axial
extension into the End
of the World
leaves it choosing
which way to turn

III.2.v.   THE MEETING OF TWO SEAS

"Is our task the less sweet / that the larvae still sleep in their cells? /
Or crawl out to attack our frail strength . . .
H.D., "Cities"

Evasive failure eviscerates
escape difficulties the Third Town
brings to the table isn't
too surprising given proximity
                     of the unspeakable girl
to ends that no longer reign
where two seas meet
             It's that kind of song
             a little blue
             but it swings

Behind the western sun
              two seas indicate ordinary
              encounters often lost to its own
              broken bustle
              measure's regulated
              dispositions
The Whole Enchilada
may be in vulgar taste but does
enrich the range of available emotion

                                   If its other is strange
                                   fluid consonants, it's still
                                   speakable but the girl

exhibits ranges of inaudible
music leaves skin abuzz
in answer to its perennial
             query

The king
lurks around the corner
wielding threatening consolidation
phantasies backed up by really
nifty order of causes prod
the Administration
into organizing the Concubines
of the Illuminati into book club's
monthly bastion
against looming empire
closeted in mind's
dark openings
into selective excisions of imperial
brutality

But longer days
are a sign even as they grow
shorter
Growing days
acknowledge her bearing
and instructions regarding
desire
City vibrates, generosity
bursting into caprice
and whim on the lintel
of day's blue vacancy

Arrangements of machine
momentary ordination
make way for the memory
of streets once dreamt,
lycanthropic shadows
stirring the alleys

                                    There
                                    at The End of the World
                                    gestures of epiphany
                                    terminate in other extensions
                        clearly indicate any point
                        of departure will do
                        as long as speculative meaning
                        lurks in vocable's
matters of fact

                        Hieroglyphic announcements
                        deflect diffusion into lapping
                        water as a kind of angelic
speech, where angelic
means something akin
                                    to coyote eyes in the dark
nameless but full
of luminous
irritant
                Birch bark morning glow
                is City's claim to other embraces
                of end just as the angular
                irruption into Bay's
                surge gladly distributes
                identity among the stars
                                    of assemblage point's
                                    emergent image story
Honey enters through text's
unexpected opening recedes
into barbershop mirror
eternities ooze from each seam
leaves City improbable
in twisted love of its streets'
passage through time

H.D.'s *larvae*

linger in light
of arrogance, a problem
of distance
though time factored
for rage

      at the first full flush
      of shoddy into every nook
      of her beloved exactitude

            (but still caught up
            in *angel's names and right*
            and wrong)

Honey is City's other
name, the always other name
the one that flashes

        in water pooled
        on cracked asphalt
        lurid radiance

              of the unnameable
angel of strip malls

III.2.VI   LUMINOUS IRRITANTS

"The wiser people boil the water down to two-thirds, add one
third of old honey, and let the mixture stand in the sun for
forty days at the time of the early rising of Sirius."
Pliny the Elder, *Natural History* XIV 113

The stakes rise in increments
of uncomfortable confrontation's
demand for clarity punctuated
by threats and clenched
metaphors wielded by aggrieved
others
  The irritation goes both
  ways, though the luminosity
  not so much

    In the Third Town
each fact irritates leaking
light from its own
skin and City is its other
     name when it's out
     on the town dancing
     to music of stellar spherical
     remains also in old Pliny's
     book
Strangers everywhere
each with a name
erased in the roar
    Other just
    being further, the Third Town
    starts to look a lot
    like Emerson's *mind*, the one
he said was common

That's democracy
if luminous irritant's grinding
in laminar clampdown's
singular assumptions conclude

                              reason's contaminating address
to falling leaves resistance
to further conclusions

                    Leave it
                    there
and democracies of spatial
potential rock four
fold shadows' temporal
thickening into deer

                    by the side of the road
                    entangled attention meandering
                    passage into furled
                    and twisted bewilderment

                                        Teeth
glisten at the margin
luminous eyes

                Wilderness lost
                in its own twists and turns
                deeper
till round dance names
its untenable border
across infoldings
of the Sirian year, up

                    from depths entered through honey
                    thieves fiery glow
                    and golden ichor of that sweet
                    blood

                          Downwind in galactic whoosh
of Sothic cycles and canicular
circuities of narrative

                significance

Embarking

is the Third Town's name
for it, redolent with H.D.'s
scent of roses and that radium

                    blue at the edge

City rambles
through it, restless now
for end's derelict

            expansion paths of honey
            laden dream and line's
            sweet order proceeds to leave

western sun behind
disposition of liquid gold
flutter over its face

            No where can do
            the who do you do
            so well, As-Ar,
            Us-Ar

                  eye star, out of the dark "A"

and "B" dance through
to scatter seeds of common

                ecstatic discriminations
                looking for place
                to be seen

                    The mystery

thickens even as who
done it paroxysms of tortured
narrative tonics and swarms
of certainty *this all has to mean*
something

        more than stone

              but can't quite say

what, contend
with resistance in bone's

            mute inoperative
            insistence on usage's passage

through distant gate
                              of horn
leading to maze at City's
root

there all along

hive
and dance, curled horn
                              furled shoot
release her, unspeakable
but lush
          in honeyed light

PART 3

Behind the western sun

"What is a value that is neither finalized nor simply equivalent to itself?"
JEAN-LUC NANCY, *THE CREATION OF THE WORLD OR GLOBALIZATION*

III.3.1   WHAT STONE MEANS

"The memory overpowers the weaker reception of *otherness* in the
'fabric of our daily acts.'"
           John Clarke, *From Feathers to Iron*

The distant thought haunts present
company anticipates expectation
                              of troubled advance

Here we go, here we go – other
images bend light around City
weigh in with pastoral
calm and tonalities suitable
for gardens of non-equivalent
                              disposition

                              Coming from beneath
                              is stone's forte, fraught with faint
                              buzz signifies shared light
                              burst from some old star's
                              heart beat lattice composition
                              still hums rare tunes
                              to sun's warmth, star
                                             to star

Tropological action unfurls
free of sin in the pull of end's
                       ends

                       The Third Town watching time
forged imposition extend into City's
                              beat, its mazed amnesia wound
and unwound around vacant
              thought of a dolmen

                                        beneath a tumulus inward
                                        and outward winding recalls
                                        honeyed light time
the music slowly breathed
the walls of Troy
                        and EP's
Dioce, star coloured terraces
intact but hard to make out
in the ashes

            Subway subway
                        subway, the chant wound up
                        in intractable appeals
                        literal passage into halls
                        of local power's winding
                                                    leads to other depths
in the Third Town's bowels

If they are all there
the three of them at last
able to hold to a meaningful
distance, why does City look
the same?
            The unspeakable
            girl may cause sharp intakes
            but another dead kid
            is its constant agony
                        Morning for lack
                        of u turns uncomfortably
                        possessed by evasion's
                        unctuous grin
There's no telling
how it is or how it ain't
what you got, it's how
it's used

Rome wasn't wrecked
in a day, they say, piling
on accumulated rubble
                              Then City
                              remembers its first kiss

and the Third Town turns
to earth and sky to see if they
can arrive
                    Arriving is in-
conclusive and in-
distinct moments of proceeding
often get there first
rendering the whole
thing as tenuous as advancing
fog across mirrored
water's blessing's
otherness we are

                    Love's scrutiny surpasses
                    knowing's clinch or at least
                    possesses it
                    though edge's
                    tendency to shift or blur
                    depends on proximity to the exit
                    as a measure of
                    propositional reliability
                    when the chips are down

Amazed in the sheer complexity
of one and one and one, accretion's
massive weight, winding
and unwinding inimical
intuition of coming poems
relishing foretaste of emerging
touch

                    The beginning
of the end of
the beginning of another one
                                        It's not
that the ground of love
is more solid than what
passes for firmament in conservative
estimates of Pleistocene projection
into accretions of sub
sequent ones
                    The dance doesn't care
                    if the stones are there
                    buzzing and buzzing
                    in implicate night

Winding passages around
and through the wall
of impassive brake lights
eternal glare, river red stasis no
ferryman can cross
to where no hungry dog waits
to greet you
                    till jewelled
towers appear in the dark
aeonic circumference
of primordial action's immaculate
line, every minute particular
entangled stone's speech

III.3.II ARCHI-SPATIALITIES OF DISPOSITION

"According to the archi-spatiality of disposition, which is also the spa-
ciousness of the opening, what's at stake is not a provenance of Being
(nor a being of provenance or of origin) but a spacing of presences."
Jean-Luc Nancy, *The experience of freedom*

"The ground of love lies *elsewhere*."
John Clarke, *From feathers to iron*

Juggled earths and stars'
     impossible sky to pin down through
         figures still an-
         nounce last

exit from instrument's bare
life returned to end
   The latest news
     poets flayed by poets
     peeled skin from muscle
     red twitch

The Third Town watches
history twist contact's
adamantine blade
   between the ribs of justice

From behind
the Western sun, now resembles
     a street sign declares
end of regulated area, the vista
     spreads into another figure
     of real encounter
     with the sentence

The Third Town hums
"The Internationale" but gets stuck on

                            we shall be all
while City writhes
          and words harden unable
          to reach each other
          in the spacious boulevards
Modular systemic
angel's names and right
and wrong determine spacing
of possession
         The end
of the world shifts gears
into ordering interventions
righteous convulsive finale
             Zombies

                 everywhere
              A sign of time's
approaching boundary freak out
by the side of an overgrown
road
     The big picture staggers
under unexpected burden
of demand for an end
            to hate
            but rallies with news
of the three Towns' disposition
into pattern of broken
but distinct modulation
along points of agreement
regarding appropriate discrimination
of urban quiddities
         Behind
         the western sun
         is no place for the weak of heart
                   and minding

the gap won't help find
the maze lurking beyond eye's
claim to perfected
impositions of monarchical
anxiety
   The First Town
demands a vote, but the result
is inconclusive
     The Second Town
stretches out its arms in joyous
embrace, abstains
       leaving the Third Town to gather

the rivers

All that glory
is a euphemism City notes
every day in streets' tangled
densities and irregular
confluences which recalls
      gathered rivers to an attention
      of a post-metaphorical arrangement
      with realities of intellect
      as they reaffirm passion's
      defining stroke

Time is overrated
as a measure of getting through
      the day although thought
      necessary by some adepts
      of unusual social positions
      banned by finicky moral
      nugatory imperatives, freezing
      the whole thing in overlays
      meant to tame restless
      haphazard divagations
      into stabilized intrusions

                                        of familiar father's taut
                                        threatening smile over faded
                                        hill and dale
                                                        City riven
by old trails slice across
scars of conquest bleeds
out of post-metaphorical
necessity to remember
the Alamo
                in sepia tones
                                No quarter asked
                                                or given is a sign, though riven
obliquely is, too, and it
gathers the rivers into a surprise
gift of connections, whirl and eddy
backwash winding
and unwinding through
stone's chambers and halls

III.3.III   Transgressive manifests of a psychoid frontier

> "The Treasures of Heaven are not Negations of Passion, but Realities of
> Intellect from which all the Passions Emanate . .."
> William Blake, *Vision of the Last Judgment*

Having been erased, heaven
shows up on City's stoop, a little
                 rough around *terrain vague's*
                 inevitable rubble and badly
                 in need of a garden

Gardens and pirates
pop up repeatedly
in unseemly festivities around such
sketchy locales, especially
after the end is over
             That's when stones
             begin to speak
             of Bloor and Simcoe, random
             instances of beer and war crisscrossed
             over their spiral heart
                         Hence heaven's
                         treasures in the gutter

Outrage and pain of broken
Sampo woven into heart tissue
breath, shredded song
             in abandoned mills

Circling bodies wind
and unwind, dance for the first
time into galleries
         of stone
             The Third Town
             shows up to recommend
             a book on Crete before leaving

for the coast of some new
found land of mundane
exchange

Indeterminate
pasts haunt its instruments
leaving up in the air
as operative mode even
as erroneous translations
put *solid* at the mercy
of *expanse* in official Syriac
delirium

Then numerical considerations
enter to shade the sense of winding
trip back to flounder
Dog totem's clue through inner
sanctuaries

It gets dark in there
but numbers shine or at least
pretend to in that rhythmic
adventure counts out steps
lead winding
and unwinding round City's root
passage through stone
galleries to light of common
story

If it's good enough
for Ishmael, it's good enough
for *I*

A common refrain
of interstitial instance's claim
to root in the face of negentropic
rumours of propositional
spread

Along with Three
Towns, City makes four, numeric
expansion takes it to another

dimension of green, further distinction
enlightened in tropological
register of each blade and leaf

        Each body's weave
        and tangled passage
        Each
        face beyond the edge

Who made that four
was one in one
of those strange
number dances
animate stone's heart
beat of sun's code's
extension in stuff's intimate
touch

    Crucial then in distanced
    synch, so that frontier
    manifests of unruly love
    order the day now brought
    to its senses, reeling through fragrant
    lily drenched air, drunk
    as a skunk raring to go

        A mind
        of its own devising
        rewards syntactic deflections with vistas
        of unprecedented trembling
        relation

            arena and neighbourhood ice
            underground chambers

                of interdimensional sound
                excursions beyond the ninth
                sphere

        inside the Administration's
        system of momentary irregular
        incursions and stacked chambers
        of machine's intricate human

workings, tension and terror
and outside living
on the grate in the heart
of wounded, feverish
earth

Skinned poets
ripen in the sun and City
weeps at the contraction
of green into enclosures
leave quest for a garden confused
with trips to the zoo

If the senses are nothing
but *modifications of the agon*
of thought, who will sing
the way home to the
world's end where action
leaves City bewildered

in whirlwind intoxication
story of multiple ecstasies in sky's
churn and wheel, the full
spread of impossible contradiction
erupts in the spacing of all
these little heres

III.3.IV VERTIGO OF THE PRODIGALITY

"Golgonooza, the spiritual four-fold London eternal
In immense labours and sorrows, ever building, ever falling"
William Blake, *Milton*

It turns out journey forged
words temporal hardening
in distant furnace and laid
out stones in air toward this
garden
       was an untoward festivity
       mingling in streets of often tenuous
       contact with further expansions
       of home

Mermaids cheer
       Mountains quiver
              Coyotes howl
                     Elephants do a little dance

But earth stories still paint
the death of Thebes and stone cults
lurk in dark, textual
recesses intoning City's name
       The difficult approach
       has been reassessed from time to time
       out, the change reflected

in vertiginous breaks rend
and grind the force that through
declensions of green
articulates stunned subtleties
still recall fuse, never stopped,
confused in the green
here sings to sun's touch
in such prodigalities

of tropological enthusiasm
known as lush
                    extended
into vernacular exchanges of weather
and health as if unexpected
                                faeries
                                returned to gardens tended
on City's roofs in declaration
of independent ecstasies
                                and reenchanted numbers'
                                commitment to adding up
beyond the sum often proposed
to regulate rowdy betweens
in the ongoing quest for stabilized
interpretations of Pluto

The Third Town giggles at the little
circling rock's name
                            finding the dark god's sudden
                            presence typical of City's
depth of field once the other two
towns have found the position necessary
to open the box
                    now containing
                                either all our woes and/or
                                an alive/dead cat
and gather the rivers into a bouquet
of times redolent with possible
extensions beyond declarations
of Babylonian determined
subway shenanigans designed to line
usual pockets of material analogy's
dramatis personae

When the cards are down
the story has them holding a royal
or busted flush as if that was the
world's end when even their own
further forms in the uproar
secretly imagine lotus
blossoms disrupted patterns
of exchange known to pave gardens
with asphalt and ignorance

Rising and falling is its name
when it is a red star
in the flames
                You are here

                Then the end begins to look
like prodigality's finality, another way
through City's mazed dream
of beginning, winding and unwinding
in stone chambers deep
in the lush letters
of its names
                the ones we will never
                know, knotting ineffable bonds
                of passing glances truncated
                smile, sudden lust

What is that faint
trace of perfumed air?

Each number, they say
                        possesses personality forged
                        from relation
                        to those around it

The city of numbers murmurs
calculations of indefinite outcome
caught in Bay's constant
surge within stone's memory

                    City hums with it, sways
slightly to implicate beat
of the mystery

The Imperium, meanwhile
                  continues to measure
                  the size of its apparatus
                  in preparation to establish
                  a true inch and Pluto's final
                  astronomical status as it applies
                  to future determinations
                  of an astro-cartological reality fix

City gets it, numbers
and all, *roil* being the name
it pulls out when the end starts
to nag at it and no white rose
                    unfolds to claim the sky
                    for its own kingdom given the dismal
                    fate of kings as an operative feature
and consequent angelic eruption
into aleatory configurations
of unexpected arrivals
from parts unknown
                  If it's right it's
wrong, and so the not-whole
shebang of its dizzy assembly
totters in joy
        at the thought
of another

III.3.V   THE LITTLE UNSPEAKABLE GIRL SHOWS HERSELF

"There is no mystery. There is an unspeakable girl."
Giorgio Agamben, *The Unspeakable Girl*

Looking for City in all
the wrong places has been
an ear worm of sorts, reminder
                              it's nowhere is an obvious
                              evasion leads untoward
                              aspects of the material analogy's
                              strangle hold on psychoid tracheal
                              flows and labyrinthine sentences
                              to syntactical boneyard

Hold your breath past
death's miasma then pick
up the tempo
                 No mystery there, though City
                 in all its mazed precincts
                 forgets to wonder where
                 she's from and where the winding
                 unwinds in the night sky

Behind the western sun
                 light recasts in softer tones
                                          to echo love's scrutiny
                                          of a familiar face, offering
                                          of honey

The dark crow virgin emerges
when the meander quaternion
embraces a sickle moon
and ensuing flutter of possible
outcomes dictates a new speech
                      syntactically irrepressible, among columns

of City's lingering link
to the Three Town's subway
transmutation, winding
and unwinding in star's whirled
stammer through dark chambers
of night's division
into words of power

Here and there she
brushes against light
opening particular renews
rise and fall of moon and sun's
harmolodic dos-a-dos
familiar story of modulation's
suggestions of even
more folding and unfolding
looking a lot like winding's
incestuous linguistic darling

Democracy can be a problem
in light of that old
Sultanism of the brain
Ishmael saw in doomed ship's
fabled structures of father
knows best wet dream, eager
to go deep and dark
Then there's the sky
sculpted procession of white's
invisible condensed body's
roiling drift, enough grandeur to further
condense a white whale
in its dark scudding folds

Story has it she shed her rosemary
scent, initiate to shadows'
hole and end after
                            end of her own entangled green
                            riven generosities

City hums
                    with a sudden inoperable thrill
                    even as it writhes
                    bloody in some dark alley
                                            The Third Town

                    calls that anagogical
                    exuberance and relishes cruelty's
                    change of heart, a process that winds
                    or unwinds, penetrant nudging
                    out penitent in circulation
of her silence through burgeoning
floral eruption's downward
orientation where rising
multitude of singular together
passes sign at the boundary
past which announcements of terminal
finality flutter uselessly in breeze
out of the wild blue yonder
returned for the finale
                            that *over there* leads to galactic
                            syntactics and *circulus lactaeus*
                            flowing through each silent
                            heart beating in maze's
                            accumulated density and white
                            spread of suckling destiny
                            through depths of demented
                            firmament

The end
is no pushover, it seems

Armageddon having lost something
in translation
        material analogy's
        ever ready flim-flam gala super show
        pyrotechnic extravaganza switch
        for just another body
        stuttering in a dark
        doorway opens on street's
                        maze
                              never ceases to appeal
                              to faint-hearted or just a little
                              mesmerized, responsive flow
choked into laminar fascination mode
even though real battles
to get back to Armageddon
                    upstream
several lines from here
                never far from home
        looks a lot like
        cavernous entrance to a
        world of cheap stuff
        down endless aisles of want

III.3.VI   WORLD'S END

"These are the chronicles / of an imaginary / town /
placed on an island / close to the shore."
Charles Olson, *Maximus Poems* 2.102

Not being here yet
is the already anticipated
measure of its
                    refrain
Never is as never
does and having an end already
is never an issue although it issues
in others past the regime
of ends
          The three Towns, already saved and lost,
          already astray past redemption's
          pretense of obligatory
          error into expansive zone where once
          having found itself
          upon a time, decides
          non-central relocation
          may provide the requisite
          prodigality to get to the next
          habitation

                    Habit is no mere slip
                    but reeks of home in rooms
                    of luminous order
                    crushed, bruised colours
                    misplaced reference

Endeavours are part of it, each
absence leaves a residue
of effort to yield trees or
pillars all juiced up
connecting the three Towns
to a distant memory or maybe
a further intimation
                         in any case
                         the world's end
                                            It glows
even on laundry day, lotus
implications spreading, and doesn't work worth a damn, testament
to end's continuing fascination
with zones and numbered precincts
nimbus extends north south
east west, the lost rivers
Don, Humber, Garrison, Taddle
flowing around and through
forgotten earth
                    The gathered rivers join
                    in a quick chorus of Moonlight
                    Becomes You before moving on
                    toward vague deltas
                    of irresolution but intensified

                                            synchronous gamma frequency
                                            oscillations and further encounters
                                            with wind in previously unsuspected
                                            crevices and folds

Arm in arm the three Towns
do a little soft shoe shuffle
while radiant extremities of the moment
seek time
            to alight in each
                              little gesture

Behind the western sun it's called
when the end remembers *erotic*
                automatism in folded plies
                of vision and gets on with
                the turbulence of merge

If you thought it was all
faerie dust and dancing
electric blue edges, you missed
                the fine print

The world's end never
            sees it coming, never
            knows what hit it, always
            winds up bruised and beating
            the band out of
            enthusiastic
corners, carrying on as if dancing
was just another treatise
              on angel magic or the mechanics
              of splendour, lotus maze in City's
              heart, winding and unwinding
vision flicker in sunflash
              off soaring glass tower
on stone's metaphorical
immensity murmuring
of star light while
just down the street
            the eternal basketball game
            proceeds and songs pour
            out someone's hidden window

The Concubines of the Illuminati argue
                  over directions to the world's
                  end, miss their turn
                  wind up in Etobicoke
                  looking for a street car

But divagation's just another name

for return to the end
of the regime of ends and they
are soon parted from all instruments
of syntactical clarity, left adrift
to recall pirate utopias
among exurban attenuations

of mental war into sudden knife flash
muzzle blast, even the death
of beauty embraced as measure
of material analogy's arid
contraction into Eglinton
at 5

   though the Third Town

            will tell whoever listens that even
there a terrible form of it
lingers in certain light in which
ever building, ever falling
wind and unwind in stone chambers

                  hollowed of words firmament yields
                  sky, stony earth
uproar of its disposition

            of archi-spatialities into untoward
            festivities beyond the western
            sun's last gasp approach
weaving, dodging through all those
vertiginous prodigalities
of the end

Michael Boughn has published numerous books of poetry including *Iterations of the Diagonal, Dislocations in Crystal, One's own Mind, 22 Skidoo/SubTractions, Cosmographia—a post-Lucretian faux micro-epic* (short listed for the Canadian Governor General's Award for Poetry in 2011), *Great Canadian Poems for the Aged Vol. 1 Illus. Ed.*, as well as a crime novel, *Business AS Usual*. With Victor Coleman, he edited Robert Duncan's *The H.D. Book*. He lives in Toronto.

ROOTS & BRANCHES SERIES TITLES ARE MADE POSSIBLE
IN PART THROUGH THE GENEROUS CONTRIBUTIONS OF

Thaddeus Rutkowski
Lynzee
Lori J. Anderson-Moseman
Richard Martin
Lee Slonimsky
Elayna Browne
Kenneth B. Nemcosky
Barbara Henning
Katy Masuga
James A. Reiss
Elizabeth J. Coleman
K. Feather Hastings
Susan Lewis
Michael Boughn
Karen Gunderson
William Luvaas
Stephen Sartarelli
Gordon Osing
Maximilian W. Valerio
Andrea Scrima
Lewis Warsh
Vitaly Chernetsky
Kathy Conde
j/j hastain
Andrew K Peterson
Marc Estrin
Gloria Frym
Marc Vincenz
Michael Forstrom

Made in the USA
Columbia, SC
10 June 2017